Intermediate

Message
Delivered

Paragraph Writing and Presentation

Leonid Yoffe
Atsuko Nishimura
Fumiko Okudaira
Mai Satake
Akira Morita

NAN'UN-DO

このテキストの音声を無料で視聴（ストリーミング）・ダウンロードできます。自習用音声としてご活用ください。
以下のサイトにアクセスしてテキスト番号で検索してください。

https://nanun-do.com　テキスト番号 [512032]

※ 無線 LAN（WiFi）に接続してのご利用を推奨いたします。

※ 音声ダウンロードは Zip ファイルでの提供になります。
　お使いの機器によっては別途ソフトウェア（アプリケーション）
　の導入が必要となります。

Message Delivered <Intermediate> 音声ダウンロードページは
左記の QR コードからもご利用になれます。

はしがき

　本書 *Message Delivered <Intermediate>* は、Paragraph Writing から Presentation へとつなげることによって学習者の発信力を強化するレベル別英語教材のひとつとして作成されました。学習者の習熟度に応じて編纂された本シリーズの共通した主な意図と特徴は次の通りです。

1. Paragraph Writing の基礎、つまりその書式 (format) 、構造 (structure)、使うべき表現 (expressions) をきちんと身に着ける。
2. それらを的確に使いながら、英語の論理構成 (logic) と展開法 (organization) にのっとり的確に自分の考えを伝えることができる。
3. しっかりとした Writing の基本を身に着けまとめられた自分の考え、意見を同じ論理構成を持った Presentation の形として口頭で発表できる。
4. Presentation の要点を、発表者 (presenter) として Presentation を行うことによって学ぶだけでなく、より重要な聴衆 (audience) の視点からの反省によって身に着ける
5. これらに加えて、特に発信にとって重要な文法項目について整理を行う。

　これらは英語の skill の面での学習の要点にもなるわけですが、それが本シリーズの最終的な目標ではありません。最終的な目標は、

a. 論理的な議論の展開（場合によっては日本語のそれとは違った）方法の基礎を知ること
b. その論理の展開法を用いて物事を考え、自分の考えを、説得力を持って効率的に、そして正確に audience に伝えられ、同時にそうできるという自信を得ること
c. 根拠を持った発言により、audience から信頼を得、グローバル人材の備えるべき発信面での能力向上を図ること

　というものです。こうした目標を、本シリーズは学習者の習熟度に合わせたレベル別の構成によって、無理なく達成できるように企画されました。

　その中で、本書 *Message Delivered <Intermediate>* は、基礎を踏まえ、より英語として自然に、また Presentation では裏付けとなる資料等にも配慮しながら、より内容的にも説得力のある Paragraph を書き Presentation が行えるようタスクの求めるものに工夫こらしています。これによって、Paragraph から Short Essay へ、より信頼性のある Presentation への発展は比較的容易なものであるはずです。そうした発展は、学習者の皆さんが、実際に何度も書き、発表することで体験しながら行ってください。それが著者一同の望みです。

　なお、刊行にあたっては、株式会社南雲堂の加藤敦さんに企画段階から多くの助言をいただきました。加藤さんの忍耐力なくしては、本シリーズの完成はなかったでしょう。また、中原緑さんには、内容の点検も含め最終的な編集場面でご面倒をお掛けしました。この場を借りて御礼申し上げます。

著者一同
2019 年盛夏

本書の使い方

本書 *Message Delivered* <*Intermediate*> では、到達目標として以下を掲げています。

1. Paragraph Writing の基礎を学び、100 ～ 120 語の Paragraph を書けるようにすること。
2. Paragraph を効果的な Presentation として口頭発表ができること。
3. 読み手 (reader) や聞き手 (audience) を意識した Paragraph を書き、Presentation ができること。

本書の構成は次の通りです。

Part I（Unit 1-4）　　Paragraph の書式 (format)、構造 (structure) を学びます。
Part II（Unit 5-10）　Paragraph の論理構成 (logic)、展開法 (organization) を学びます。
Part III（Unit 11-14）Presentation の要点と効果的な発表の仕方について学びます。

それぞれの Part には様々なタスクがありますが、それぞれの意図を参考に各自が予習・復習などの学習計画を組み立ててください。

Warm Up

アンケートやブレーンストーミング形式の問題に答えて、各 Unit で扱うトピックについての知識や考えを整理します。"How did the Internet change our lives?"（Unit 5 より）などの質問について、他の学習者と意見交換することにより、更にトピックに対する考えを深めます。様々な考えや情報を書き出しておくことにより、Unit の後半で Outline や Writing a Paragraph を書く際の材料となります。

Paragraph Analysis

各 Unit で扱う構造や論理構成、展開法について学びます。まず、Topic Sentence や Supporting Sentence などの用語の定義と実例を確認していきます。さらに Unit の重要項目の観点から Exercises A・B の Model Paragraph を分析して知識の定着を図ります。ここで用いられる表現や語句を使えるようにしていきましょう。また、論理構成や展開の仕方も Model Paragraph の中でどうなっているかを理解したうえで Outline や Writing a Paragraph の課題につなげていきますので、しっかりと学習内容を身につけて書けるようにしてほしいところです。

Grammar for Writing

英文を書くときに注意しておきたい文法項目をまとめました。時制の使い分けや助動詞の意味、接続詞（特に従属接続詞と副詞節など）、形容詞と副詞などの基本的な項目を再確認し、実際に英文を書くときに参考にしてもらいたい内容です。選択式、書き換え、整序作文などの形で理解度を測っていますが、まず参考書や辞書で該当する文法用語、例文は調べておくことが望ましいです。

Useful Vocabulary for the Topic

　各 Unit のトピックに関する語（句）の正しい意味を選択肢から選びます。次のセクションで自分自身のパラグラフの概要を作成する際、このセクションで学んだ語彙が役に立つので、語義を確認すると共に、英語でも言える（書ける）ようにしましょう。モデル・パラグラフで学んだ語彙の関連語（例：benefit ➡ beneficial）が含まれる場合もあるので、モデル・パラグラフの語彙と併せて覚えると、より効果的です。

Outline

　これまで学んできた Paragraph の構造や展開法を実際に書くための準備段階です。図表などに自分の考えていることを書いていく中で書く内容を整理していきます。語句レベルでのまとめから丁寧に学んできた文法項目などを使いながら一文、一文形にしていくプロセスを大事にしてください。

Writing a Paragraph

　Outline でまとめた内容を Paragraph の形に直していく課題です。英文の構造と内容の理解をもとに、特に主語、動詞、目的語、補語の形式と機能、修飾関係に注意を払って書く訓練をするとよいでしょう。

Your Own Presentation

　Part III では Unit 10 で書いた Paragraph を Presentation 用の原稿に書き換えていきます。Presentation で用いる表現に気をつけ自分で実際に声を出しながら、また Presentation 用のスライドを使いながら話す練習につなげていきます。また、相手に聞いてもらうように話すことと、人の発表を注意深く聞く練習も含まれていますので、学習者が相互に評価しながらすすめるとよいでしょう。

（注）本書ではキーワードとなる用語については英語表記にしています。

Contents

UNIT 1　Paragraphの構造

Formatting（書式）

　効率よく情報を伝達するには、決められた書式（Formatting）にそって文章を作成しなければなりません。学術的な文章を雑誌等に投稿する場合でも、それぞれの投稿先によって、書式が決められています。本書では、以下の書式にそってパラグラフ（Paragraph）の作成を行います。なお、以下の書式は、ワープロソフトで作成することを前提にしていますが、手書きの場合もこれに準じて作成しましょう。

title：最初の行にタイトルを書く。中央揃えにして、すべての単語の最初の文字を大文字にする。ただし、冠詞、前置詞、接続詞、代名詞などは、タイトルの先頭以外では小文字にする。

name and date：ヘッダーに右寄せで名前と提出日を記入する

indentation：最初の文は3～5文字程度、右側に字下げをする。

line space：十分な行間を取る。目安は1行おきの行間。ワープロソフトの場合、行数を25行程度に設定する。

margin：上下左右に十分な余白を設定する。目安は、およそ以下の通り。
　上 35mm
　下 30mm
　左右 35mm

line break：語の途中での改行はできるだけ避ける。また、1つの文ごとに改行するようなことはしない。

alignment：配置は「両端揃え」もしくは、「左揃え」にする。

font：Century や Times New Roman が一般的。本文の文字サイズは12ポイント程度の見やすいサイズにする。タイトルは本文よりも少し大きなサイズにする。

paper：A4用紙

Kato Atsushi
April 13, 20XX

Ruth Bader Ginsburg

　There are three female Supreme Court justices in the U.S. as of September 2019. Ruth Bader Ginsburg is one of them. She is one of the best known advocates of gender equality and human rights. She won many cases during her long career. And some of her legal victories had a very profound impact on American society. For example, the male-only admissions policy of the Virginia Military Institute was abolished in 1996 as a result of her efforts. Now she is 86 years old, the oldest of the nine justices. Because of her advanced age and health issues many people assumed she would be retiring. However, Ruth Ginsburg said she would remain on the Supreme Court and continue fighting to make America a better country for all.

以下の Paragraph について、書式上の問題点を指摘しましょう。

> In 2018 the Japanese government made casinos legal.
>
> However, some experts, including medical doctors and social workers have opposed this plan.
>
> One reason is that it may increase the number of people addicted to
>
> gambling. Gambling addiction can result in serious personal and social
>
> problems, such as unemployment, debts, and the collapse of family.
>
> Another reason for their opposition is that gambling may lead to a higher crime rate.
>
> We have seen evidence of a connection between casinos and organized crime. Unfortunately,
>
> Japan already has the largest number of people with gambling addiction in the world.
>
> Eighty percent of them are addicted to pachinko slot machines.
>
> Obviously, we still need, more debate before implementing this plan.

Paragraph Structure

　一つの話題について述べているいくつかの文のまとまりのことを Paragraph（パラグラフ）と言います。Paragraph は、以下の構成要素が順序良く並べられることによって読者に伝わりやすくなるとされています。

① Introductory Sentence（導入文）
　　Paragraph の話題に関する背景や一般的な事柄を示し、通常 Paragraph の先頭に置かれる。

② Topic Sentence（主題文）
　　Paragraph の話題とその話題に対する筆者の考えを提示する。

③ Supporting Sentences（支持文）
　　Topic Sentence で提示した考えがいかに正しいのかを、具体例や理由などを示して、裏付ける文。具体例や理由などの数に応じて、複数の支持文を置くことになる。

④ Details（ディテール）
　　支持文に続いて、支持文の補足をする文。それぞれの支持文に 1 ～ 2 文加えるのが普通。

⑤ Concluding Sentence（まとめの文）
　　支持文の内容をまとめたり、主題文の主張を別のことばで言い換えたりして Paragraph 全体をまとめる文。Paragraph の最後に置かれる。

＊ 本書では、① Introductory Sentence（1 文）＋②主題文（1 文）＋③支持文（2 ～ 3 文）＋④ Details（2 ～ 3 文）＋⑤まとめの文（1 文）からなる Paragraph を書く練習をしていきます。Paragraph によっては、①の Introductory Sentence を省略し、②の Topic Sentence から書き始める場合もあります。

Kato Atsushi
April 13, 20XX

Ruth Bader Ginsburg

① There are three female Supreme Court justices in the U.S. as of September 2019 (Introductory Sentence).　② Ruth Bader Ginsburg is one of them (Topic Sentence). ③ -A: She is one of the best known advocates of gender equality and human rights (Supporting Sentence 1). ④ -A: She won many cases during her long career (Detail 1). ③ -B: And some of her legal victories had a very profound impact on American society (Supporting Sentence 2). ④ -B: For example, the male-only admissions policy of the Virginia Military Institute was abolished in 1996 as a result of her efforts (Detail 2). ③ -C: Now she is 86 years old, the oldest of the nine justices (Supporting Sentence 3).
④ –C: Because of her advanced age and health issues many people assumed she would be retiring (Detail 3).　⑤ However, Ruth Ginsburg said she would remain on the Supreme Court and continue fighting to make America a better country for all (Concluding Sentence).

---

① Topic の背景となる共有すべき情報（米国最高裁の女性判事）について触れて導入しています。
② Topic のルース・ベイダー・ギンズバーグを紹介しています。
③ -A, B & C と④ -A, B & C　Topic について詳しく具体的に述べています。
⑤ 最後にギンズバーグについて伝えたいポイントを簡潔にまとめています。

次の Paragraph を読み、後の問に答えましょう。

In 2018 the Japanese government made casinos legal. However, some experts, including medical doctors and social workers, have opposed this plan. One reason is that it may increase the number of people addicted to gambling. Gambling addiction can result in serious personal and social problems, such as unemployment, debts, and the collapse of family. Another reason of their opposition is that gambling may lead to a higher crime rate. We have seen evidence of a connection between casinos and organized crime. Unfortunately, Japan already has the largest number of people with gambling addiction in the world. Eighty percent of them are addicted to pachinko slot machines. Obviously, we still need more debate before implementing this plan.

1. Paragraph の話題に関する背景や一般的な事柄として示されている導入文の内容を説明しましょう。

2. Paragraph の Topic は何ですか。

3. Topic についての具体例や理由として最初に挙げられていることは何ですか。

4. 3を補足するためにどのようなことが書かれていますか。

5. Topic についての具体例や理由として2つ目に挙げられていることは何ですか。

6. 5を補足するためにどのようなことが書かれていますか。

7. Topic についての具体例や理由として3つ目に挙げられていることは何ですか。

8. 7を補足するためにどのようなことが書かれていますか。

9. まとめ（結論）の一文にはどのようなことが書かれていますか。

Exercise C

次の Paragraph を読み、Title、Introductory Sentence、Topic Sentence、3 つの Supporting Sentences、3 つの Details、Concluding Sentence の内容を、囲みの中から選んで空欄に記入しましょう。

🎧 4

The Hispanic population has been growing in the U.S. What does the word "Hispanic" mean in the U.S.? Firstly, the term "Hispanic" usually refers to people from Latin America, and they are also called Latinos. "Hispanic" is officially mentioned by the U.S. Government while "Latino" is sometimes used by Latinos-themselves with a sense of ethnic pride. Secondly, "Hispanic" refers to Spanish-speaking people. Therefore, people from Brazil are not regarded as Hispanic although they come from Latin America. Thirdly, "Hispanic" is a term to indicate their ethnicity or culture, rather than their race. It is because this term includes diverse races: Caucasians, African Americans, and even Native Americans. To sum up, in the U.S. the word "Hispanic" means Spanish speakers from Latin America regardless of their race.

Title: ....

Introductory Sentence の内容 : ....

Topic Sentence の内容 : ....

Supporting Sentence 1 の内容 : ....

Detail 1 の内容 : ....

Supporting Sentence 2 の内容 : ....

Detail 2 の内容 : ....

Supporting Sentence 3 の内容 : ....

Detail 3 の内容 : ....

Concluding Sentence の内容 : ....

Brazilians ≠ Hispanics
Hispanics = Spanish speakers from Latin America
Hispanics = people from Latin America
Hispanics in the U.S.
"Hispanic" ➡ ethnicity / culture
What "Hispanic" means in the U.S.
"Hispanic" ➡ officially used, "Latino" ➡ ethnic pride
various races among Hispanics
Hispanics speak Spanish.
Hispanic population in the U.S.

Grammar for Writing

[Sentence Structure] 文の構造

文の構造の3タイプ
英文には3つのタイプがあります。

1. 単文：S + V の関係が一つだけで、主節のみで成り立っている文
   I like coffee.
   The Earth goes around the Sun.
   Mary did not go to the party.

2. 重文：2つ以上の節が等位接続詞やセミコロンで結ばれた文
   I like coffee and Mary likes tea.
   Mary went to work but came home soon.
   Our car broke down; we came last.

3. 複文：主節と従属節が従位接続詞や関係詞で結ばれた文
   We missed our plane because we got stuck in a traffic jam.
   Our dog barks when she hears a noise.
   Do you know the man who is talking to Mary?

Exercise D

空欄に接続詞や関係詞を補って各文を完成しましょう。

1. Hurry up, (   ) you'll be late for the meeting.
2. I don't care (   ) I do well on that test or not.
3. He went (   ) he could find work.
4. She didn't water the plant, (   ) it managed to survive until she came back from vacation.
5. I get Cs in math (   ) in history I usually get straight As.

| while wherever or yet if |

Exercise E

次の和文を英文に直しましょう。

1. 私の英語は通じなかった。(make oneself understood を用いた単文)

2. それはとても良い考えですね。(sound like を用いた単文)

3. そのパーティーにはあまり知り合いがいなかったが、彼女は楽しんでいた。
   (enjoy oneself を用いた複文)

4. 彼は、公表されるまで結婚のことを秘密にしていた。(keep...secret を用いた複文)

5. 雨が降るでしょう、空が非常に暗いですから。(overcast を用いた複文)

UNIT 2 Topic Sentenceとは

　Topic Sentence には 話題とその話題について何を述べるのかが提示されます。通常 Paragraph の Main idea となる topic と assertion（主張）、そして limitation（制限）または condition（条件）で 1 文が構成されます。limitation (condition) を付加することによって主張の範囲を限定することができますが、topic と assertion のみで提示されることもあります。一般に Topic Sentence は先頭にきますが、Paragraph の話題にかかわる背景などを紹介する Introductory Sentence（導入文）から始まる場合は Topic Sentence は 2 番目に置かれます。読み手がその Paragraph は何について書かれているかを即座に理解できるようにわかりやすい Topic Sentence を書くことを心掛けましょう。また Topic Sentence にその主張を支持する理由がその後いくつ述べられるかを加えて全体の方向性を示すこともあります。

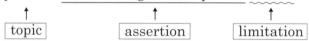

· **My sister** is the most generous person I know.

· **Eating healthy foods** offers four concrete benefits.

· **Walking** is the best way to explore an unfamiliar town for three reasons.

Tips for a Better Topic Sentence

　Topic Sentence の内容はあまり漠然とさせず、また具体的過ぎないようにしましょう。

漠然としている例： The internet has changed the world.
→ especially for the young generation / especially for business などを付加しましょう。

具体的過ぎる例： In Singapore the birthrate changed from 1.6 to 1.2 children per woman between in 2000 and 2019.
→ 読者が展開を予測しやすいよう、The declining birthrate is a serious social problem in Singapore now. などと変えましょう。

次の文の topic を□で囲み、assertion に下線を付けましょう。

1. Living with your parents has several advantages.

2. My cousin had a very scary experience at work one day.

3. Time management at the time of exams is quite important.

4. A successful journey requires a lot of preparation.

Exercise B

次の文の topic を□で囲み、limitation に下線を付けましょう。

1. A library is the best place for students to study quietly.

2. Taking a moderate exercise is effective to relieve stress.

3. Art therapy is becoming a popular treatment for many emotional disorders.

4. Sustainable energy is a top priority in many developing nations.

Exercise C

例にならって Topic Sentence をより効果的になるように limitation[condition] を付け加えましょう。

(Ex) Working part-time is a good idea.

Working part-time is good for university students.

1. Exercise improves health.

2. The government introduced a new policy.

3. Many tourists come to Japan.

4. Studying abroad is essential.

5. Hawaii is a popular destination.

Exercise D

次の topic に assertion, limitation（condition）を書き加えて Topic Sentence を完成させましょう。

例 [topic]　　　　　　　　Computer

　[assertion+limitation]　Computers have changed not only the way we do business but also how we communicate with each other.

1. Travelling overseas

2. Soccer

3. Friends

4. Assignment

5. Work experience

次の英文に適切な Topic Sentence を書きましょう。

Smartphones can help children stay in touch with their parents in case of emergency. However, the use of smartphones is not problem-free. Children can become victims of online fraud, for example. To prevent this from happening, parents should monitor how their children use their phones.

Grammar for Writing

現在形 ［Simple Present］

現在形の用法

1. 習慣的な動作や持続的な性質や状態を表現する時には現在形を用います。
   My father writes for a local newspaper.

2. 一般的な事実や真理について述べる際にも現在形を使います。
   Water is essential for our life.

3. 一般動詞の現在形には動詞の原形を使いますが、主語が三人称単数の場合には原形の語尾に -(e)s をつけます。
   He always studies hard, especially before an exam.

4. 時や条件を表す副詞節では未来の事柄を示すために現在形を使用します。
   Let's ask her about it when she comes back.

＊文を作る時には主語と動詞が正確に呼応しているかに留意しましょう。

Exercise F

動詞を適切な形に変え当てはめて文を完成させましょう。

1. Our teacher (　　　　　　　) Swedish fluently.

2. Russia and Norway (　　　　　　　) a border.

3. My favorite bands (　　　　　　　) at local festival every year.

4. The dog (　　　　　　) at strangers.

5. Call me when you (　　　　　　) New York.

| reach | speak | own | bark | share | perform |

Exercise G

次の英文の誤りを適切に直しましょう。

My brothers is athletes. Thomas is a good tennis player and Kenneth are good at swimming because they practices non-stop. They also trains young kids on weekends. Their enthusiasm always encourage kids to do their best.

現在形を用いて文を完成させましょう。

1. Careful cyclists

2. Foreign tourists

3. My hometown

4. One of my friends

5. A good restaurant

UNIT 3 Supporting Sentence とは

Supporting Sentences は Topic Sentence で紹介された話題について付加的に説明をする役目を果たします。単に Topic Sentence の言い換えをするわけではなく、main idea（主題）をより分かりやすく説明し、読み手を説得するために必要な topic に沿った新しい情報を与える目的も担っています。

また Supporting Sentence の後に、より具体的で詳しい情報を Detail として続けることで Paragraph 全体の説得力を高めます。Supporting Sentences は定義、説明、例などを含みますが、通常１文ではなく２文以上となることが多く、それぞれの文について Detail を１文または２文以上付加することが一般的です。その際似通った情報を取りまとめながら、First, Second, Third, Lastly などといった語を使って、順序良く提示するようにしましょう。

Topic Sentence: A smartphone is effective in case of emergency.
Supporting Sentence (1): You can have access to the up-to-date information about a disaster.
Detail (1):   For example, you can check the train service and decide what to do.
Supporting Sentence (2): You can find an evacuation facility nearby and also contact your family.
Detail (2):   You may be able to move to a safe location quickly.

＊ Supporting Sentence は常に topic に関わる事物を挙げて、Cohesion（一貫性）を持って書くことが求められます。
　△ A smartphone helps us to communicate with people in the local community. (Irrelevant)

Exercise A

次の文の中から Topic Sentence (TS)、Supporting Sentence (SS)、Detail (D) を探してみましょう。

1. [   ] Excessive use of smartphone leads to health problems.
   [   ] For example, our eyesight gets weaker and we may suffer from a lack of sleep.
   [   ] Young people are becoming too dependent on smartphones.

2. [   ] It can help people move around.
   [   ] Improving public transportation produces concrete economic benefits.
   [   ] People enjoy shopping and going out.

3. [   ] Then you have to check recipes for a healthy diet.
   [   ] There are two steps to follow in order to lose weight.
   [   ] First you need to decide your ideal weight and plan your exercise routine.

次の Topic Sentence を読み Supporting Sentence として適切な文に◎を Detail として適切な文に
○をつけましょう。

1. Topic Sentence: Living in the countryside is enjoyable in many ways.
   - [   ]   We can enjoy clean air and the natural environment.
   - [   ]   Life in rural areas can be extremely boring.
   - [   ]   People living in rural areas spend less money on housing than city residents.
   - [   ]   We can buy fresh vegetables directly from farmers.

2. Topic Sentence : Hybrid cars are ecofriendly and economical.
   - [   ]   They produce lower emissions than ordinary cars.
   - [   ]   They typically run on electricity rather than gasoline.
   - [   ]   Not many people can afford to buy a hybrid car because they are still quite expensive.
   - [   ]   They can reduce CO_2 by 25%, compared to diesel cars.

Exercise C

次の Topic Sentence に続く Supporting Sentence と Detail を考えてみましょう。

1. Smoking should be banned entirely in all public spaces.

   Supporting Sentence:

   Detail:

2. Many of Japanese popular foods are healthy.

   Supporting Sentence:

   Detail:

3. People in cities tend to be indifferent to others.

   Supporting Sentence:

   Detail:

4. There are three steps to follow to ensure a successful trip.

Supporting Sentence:

Detail:

5. Bullying at a workplace is one of social problems.

Supporting Sentence:

Detail:

Exercise D

次の英文を読み設問に答えましょう。

Silver

Silver, a precious metal, is treasured for several reasons. Firstly, silver is relatively rare and has a distinctive color. As a result, it has been extensively used to make coins and for jewelry since ancient times. Secondly, certain properties of silver make it very useful for industrial applications. For example, silver is used in solar panels, smartphones and other advanced technologies. The medical industry relies on silver as well. As you can see, silver is valued not only for its beauty but also its special qualities as a rare natural resource.

1. Topic を□で囲み assertion に波線をつけましょう。

2. Supporting Sentence に下線を付けましょう。

3. Detail に二重線をつけましょう。

Grammar for Writing

過去形 ［Simple Past］

過去形の用法

1. 過去のある時の動作や出来事、状態を表現する時には過去形を用います。
   (last week, ago, the other day, at that time など特定の過去を示す語を伴う)
   World War Ⅱ broke out in 1939.

2. 過去の習慣的な動作、反復的出来事について述べる際にも過去形を使います。
   Whenever I went abroad, I took my son with me.

3. 主節の時制が過去になると従節は時制の一致により過去形で表現します。
   He knew that she was the first woman to become the mayor of San Francisco.

Exercise E

動詞を適切な形に変え当てはめて文を完成させましょう。

1. My essay was due yesterday, so I (   ) up late the night before.

2. While Tom was playing the guitar, one of the strings (   ).

3. Every time Laura saw me, she came running and (   ) with me for a while.

4. Our house (   ) the worst typhoon last month.

5. Last night when I was taking shower, I (   ) a loud noise outside.

| survive | hear | break | stay | talk | perform |

Exercise F

次の英文の誤りを適切に直しましょう。

Two years ago, I enroll in a sky diving course. First I was so nervous and I regret the decision. Every time I put on a harness, I have to overcome my fear. However, after I discover the real joy of sky diving, my courage beat my anxiety. Finally I notice that I truly enjoy sky diving.

Exercise G

過去の努力した経験について、出来事の前、出来事、その後について書いてみましょう。

A difficult situation:

Before:

During:

After:

UNIT 4 Concluding Sentenceとは

　Concluding Sentence とは Paragraph の終わりの文で、Topic をとりまとめて説明する役割を果たします。新しい情報を入れずに Supporting Sentences で述べたことを取りまとめる他に、Topic Sentence を別の言葉で言い換えて Topic を読者に再認識してもらう意図も持ちます。Concluding Sentence を in conclusion, to sum up, in brief, therefore といった語で始めることも多いですが、内容に即した効果的な語を使い、Paragraph が終わりへと向かっていることを明示しましょう。また Concluding Sentence には読者に予想や注意を促すものや、意見をはっきりと示す文も含まれます。

例： **Topic Sentence:**　　　　An efficient city has three important features.

　　　Concluding Sentence: Thanks to these features, people can enjoy a comfortable life in a place like this.

予想を促す **Concluding Sentence** の例

　Therefore, detailed market research will be required for an increase in overseas sales.

注意を促す **Concluding Sentence** の例

　If you do not follow these steps, you may have trouble while traveling.

意見を述べる **Concluding Sentence** の例

　For these reasons I completely agree that there should be a penalty for underage drinking.

Exercise A

次の a 〜 b の中で Topic Sentence に対応する Concluding Sentence として適切な文を選びましょう。

1. There are three steps to finding a good accommodation online.
   a. Rates are getting higher every year,
   b. Following these steps makes it easier to find a perfect place to stay.
   c. You can save money by booking online.

2. Using credit cards can be risky for students.
   a. Students who are not good at money management can get into serious debt.
   b. Using credit cards is common among students.
   c. Some credit companies allow students to borrow large sums of money.

3. The increasing amount of violence in films is becoming a serious social problem.
   a. Such films can have a harmful effect on children.
   b. However, regulating film industry is not effective.
   c. In order to combat these problems, the government should take concrete measures immediately.

次の Concluding Sentence はどのような文でしょうか。適切なものを選びましょう。

1. Your pancakes will turn out great if you follow this recipe.
       a. prediction   b. opinion   c. warning

2. If the government is too conservative, the young people are less likely to vote in the next election.
       a. prediction   b. opinion   c. warning

3. This research can lead to a medical breakthrough in the future.
       a. prediction   b. opinion   c. warning

4. Without these measures, the population in Japan will definitely shrink.
       a. prediction   b. opinion   c. warning

5. From this work experience I gained confidence and a sense of responsibility.
       a. prediction   b. opinion   c. warning

Exercise C

次の Topic Sentence に合う Concluding Sentence を書きましょう。

1. It is important for new students to establish a social network.

2. I had a rewarding experience during my stay in America.

3. Cycling is the best way to get rid of stress.

4. The government should encourage people to recycle by taking these steps.

5. Eating together can be great for family bonding.

Exercise D

次の文を読み設問に答えましょう。

> Our university does a great deal to support overseas students. First of all, the institution offers many opportunities for foreign and domestic students to meet informally. At these events students can have a valuable language exchange, find out more about university life and local culture and, most importantly, make friends. [　①　] If, however, a foreign student wishes to live off-campus, the university can provide assistance in finding an apartment nearby. Finally, the administration of the university helps overseas students find a job after graduation. [　②　]

1. ①に適切な Supporting Sentence を書きましょう。

2. ②に適切な Concluding Sentence を書きましょう。

現在完了 ［Perfect Present］

現在完了の用法
現在完了は have[has] + 過去分詞の形をとり、次のような意味を表します。

1. 現在における動作の完了・結果

   He has not returned from Paris yet.

2. 現在までの経験

   I have been to America twice.

3. 現在までの状態の継続

   We have known each other for ten years.

4. 現在までの動作の継続

   How long have you been working here?

Exercise E

（　　　）内に適切な語を入れて文を完成させましょう。

1. Have you ever (　　　　　　　　　) abroad?

2. He has (　　　　　　) (　　　　　　　　　　) stamps since he was 10 years old.

3. I thought you have (　　　　　　　) your homework already.

4. Five years have (　　　　　　　) since we became friends.

5. It has (　　　　　　) raining for three days.

Exercise F

次の英文の誤りを直しましょう。

1. The express train has departed on schedule.

2. When have you heard the news?

3. I know Paul for six years.

4. My brother was studying since this morning.

5. My father has never gone abroad.

Exercise G

指示された語句を使って、完了形を用いて英語で表現してみましょう。

1. 私はシンガポールで地理学を3年学んでいます。
   (Singapore / geography)

2. 政府は学校のいじめ問題に真剣に取り組んできています。
   (addressed / bullying)

3. スマートフォンが国内でありふれたものになってきています。
   (commonplace / nationwide)

4. あなたはアメリカに何度行ったことがありますか。
   (how many / been)

5. アンはちょうど売り上げのレポートを書き終えたところです。
   (just / sales report)

これまで１年以上続けている習慣について現在完了形を用いて文を書いてみましょう。また継続している理由や、その方法などについてもまとめてみましょう。

_____

_____

_____

What is a good title?

● 良いタイトルには次のような特徴があります。

> 良いタイトルの特徴
> 1）読み手の興味をそそる
> 2）Paragraph の内容を想像することができる
> 3）あまり長くない（文にはしない）

● タイトルは、Paragraph を書く前に決めても、書き終わった後に決めても構いません。それぞれ次のような手法を取ることがあります。

1）Paragraph を書く前に決める場合：Paragraph の主旨（main idea）から思いつくキーワードを使って、タイトルに主旨を織り込むようにする

2）一通り書き終わった後に決める場合：Paragraph で使った重要な語句を選び、タイトルに組み込むようにする

UNIT 5 人や物について説明してみよう (Listing/Examples)

　私たちには日々の生活で人や物について説明する機会があります。相手に素早く理解してもらうためには、どのような点に注意して説明をすればよいのかを考えてみましょう。

[本課の目標]
・ 人や物等の特徴、利点等について考える。
・ Listing Paragraph
　構造・文法・語彙を理解する。(Input)
・ Outline/Paragraph を作成する。(Output)

Warm Up

A. 次のアンケートに答えましょう。

1. Whom do you admire the most?

2. What is the usefulness of AI?

3. For what purposes should AI technology be used?

4. How did the Internet change our lives?

5. What is your ideal travel destination?

B. ペアで A のアンケートを元に話し合いましょう。

Paragraph Analysis

Listing/Examples

　Topic Sentence の主張を証明するために、事物や人について具体的な例を挙げながら説明をする時に使う方法です。対象が物ならば利点や欠点などの特徴を挙げると読者が理解しやすくなります。

＜ Useful Expressions ＞

First, second, third..., One reason, another reason..., One advantage, second advantage... 事柄や例を列挙する際に ; (セミコロン) でつなぐこともできます。

例： One advantage of smartphones is easy access to the Internet.

　　　Another advantage of smartphones is large memory to store pictures.

Exercise A

次の Paragraph の構造を確認して枠内を埋めましょう。

The Benefits of Machine Translation

　Machine translation offers many benefits. The biggest benefit is speed. While a professional translator can translate on average about 2,000 words per day, a machine can handle the same number of words in less than a minute. This is important for companies which work under very tight deadlines. The second advantage is cost. Machine translation is free in many cases. You only need a computer with Internet access to download a translation application. Salaries for human translators, on the other hand, can be quite high. Finally, machine translation is available anytime and anywhere while human translators are not. Imagine that your company is urgently required to translate an important document from Swahili to Swedish in the middle of the night. Machine translation may be the only way it can be done. While there are still some problems with the quality of translation work performed by the machines, the benefits listed above make it a very attractive option for businesses, governments and ordinary people.

Topic Sentence（主題の内容）

Supporting Sentence 1 （利点①）

Detail （利点①の具体的なメリット）

Supporting Sentence 2 （利点②）

Detail （利点②の具体的なメリット）

Supporting Sentence 3 （利点③）

Detail （利点③の具体的なメリット）

Concluding Sentence （主題の確認とまとめ）

Exercise B

[　　] 内に適切な語句を入れて Paragraph を完成させましょう。

An American inventor, Thomas Edison was a very unique person. [①], he had an interesting educational background. With his mother's help, he studied by himself after quitting elementary school. He was a hard worker and was extremely curious. Some of his inventions were inspired by his work as a telegraph operator. [②], Edison was one of the prolific inventors in the world. He invented more than 1,000 devices. He invented not only the phonograph, motion picture camera, light bulb and car battery, but also a number of household devices. Edison truly left an undeniable impact on many aspects of our life and many of the conveniences we continue to enjoy today can be attributed to the brilliant mind of this great American inventor.

① _____   ② _____

Grammar for Writing

[Present Progressive] 現在進行形

現在進行形とは
現在進行している動作や行為を表すとき、近い未来について述べるときに用いる形式です。

現在進行形の形
主語＋ be 動詞の現在形＋動詞 ing

1. 現在進行中の動作
   He is installing an application on his cell for paying bills online.
   ＊状態を表す動詞はふつう進行形にしない。（have, resemble, know, like, understand など）

2. 近い未来
   He is leaving for Boston tonight.

Exercise C

和文に合うように動詞を適切な形に直しましょう。

1. Tim _____ a game on his PC. (download)
   ティムは自分のパソコンにゲームをダウンロードしています。

2. This online shop _____ the books I ordered today. (send)
   このオンラインショップは今日私が注文した本を発送する予定です。

3. That car _____ automatically using AI technology. (move)
   その車は AI の技術を使って自動で動いています。

4. Sally _____ as her friends _____ to her. (smile, wave)
   サリーは友達が手を振っているので微笑んでいます。

5. The president of the company _____ soon because of the scandals. (resign)
   その会社の社長はスキャンダルの為にもうすぐ辞任する予定です。

Exercise D

和文の意味に合うように英単語を並べ替えましょう。

1. エジソンはいまだに彼の発明品を通して私たちの日常生活に貢献しています。
   Edison [daily / still / life / to / is / our / contributing] through his innovations.

   Edison _____ through his innovations.

2. 若い夫婦に助成金を与えることが地元経済に利益を与えています。
   Giving a subsidy [married couples / benefiting / young / to / is] the local community.

   Giving a subsidy _____ the local community.

3. 人工知能の技術は障害のある人々を助けています。
   AI technology [with / helping / disabilities / is / people].

   AI technology _____ .

4. タブレットを使った学習が現在流行しています。
   Learning [booming / tablets / using / is / by] now.

   Learning _____ now.

5. 私は7日の午前中にニューヨークに着く予定です。
   I am [of / the / in / on / arriving / morning / New York] the seventh.

   I am _____ the seventh.

Useful Vocabulary for the Topic

Exercise E

次のそれぞれの語句の意味を a. 〜 j. の中から選びましょう。

_____	1. beneficial	a.	〜にまさる
_____	2. disadvantageous	b.	危機管理
_____	3. contribution	c.	自動ブレーキ
_____	4. outweigh	d.	貢献
_____	5. respectable	e.	尊敬すべき
_____	6. high-performance	f.	ゲノム医療
_____	7. eco-friendly	g.	不利な
_____	8. automatic brake	h.	環境にやさしい
_____	9. risk management	i.	高性能
_____	10. genomic medicine	j.	役に立つ

Outline

AI の利点または欠点を説明する Paragraph の Outline を作りましょう。身近にある AI を活用している物や、これから AI が医療やビジネスでの実用例なども調べて例示しましょう。

Topic（AI の利点または欠点を挙げましょう）

Supporting idea 1（一つ目の利点または欠点を示しましょう。）

Detail 1（一つ目の利点または欠点の具体的な説明を提示しましょう）

Supporting idea 2（二つ目の利点または欠点を示しましょう。）

Detail 2（二つ目の利点または欠点の具体的な説明を提示しましょう）

Writing a Paragraph

Outline をもとに Paragraph の下書きを書いてみましょう。それぞれの Supporting Sentence に Detail を書き加えましょう。

UNIT 6 まちの歴史や未来について考えてみよう（Time Order）

　世界の事象を捉える方法の一つに時系列が挙げられます。過去から現在の流れを知ることは未来予測にもつながるでしょう。

［本課の目標］
・ まちの歴史について考える。
・ Time Order Paragraph
　構造・語彙・文法を理解する。（Input）
・ Outline/Paragrah を作成する。（Output）

Warm Up

クラスメイトにインタビューをしてみましょう。

1. What is your favorite city/town/village and why?

2. When did you visit this place last?

3. What do you know about the history of this place?

4. Would you prefer to live in a big city or a small town? Why?

【Expansion activity】

「まち」に関する質問文を一つ作り、クラス内で統計をとってみましょう。

Your question:

Time Order

時間の流れに沿って述べる Paragraph のパターンです。この課では歴史に焦点をあてます。
① まちの歴史に関わる視点を Topic Sentence で示します。
② 出来事の順序を整理し、始まり・経過・現在の形を時の表現を適宜入れて記します。
③ 結語や未来への展望等を記します。

＜ Useful Expressions ＞

時を表す語彙

1450 BC / 859 AD / CE / the 13th Century / in 1920 / 1970s / Edo period / in the past / ancient times / since / until / then / after that / later / soon / when / before / around / from 1579 until 1821 / between A and B

Model Paragraph

Exercise A

次の Paragraph の構造や歴史の流れを確認しましょう。

The History of the Island of Santorini

The Island of Santorini, a popular travel destination in Greece, has a long and fascinating history. In ancient times, the Minoans settled in the south-western end of the island. However, around 1450 BC, the volcano on the island erupted and the area was buried. Nobody lived there for centuries until the 13th century BC. In the 9th century BC, a small village was established on the clifftop. Later, Santorini was ruled by the Romans and the Byzantines. The Turks controlled the island from 1579 until 1821, when Greece became independent. Only then did Santorini become part of Greece. It is widely considered to be one of the most beautiful islands in the world and it will continue to attract tourists from everywhere.

Topic Sentence: _____

> 始まり

⬇

> 経過

⬇

> 現在・未来

Concluding Sentence: _____

次の Paragraph の「時を表す語」を抜き出し、時系列を確認し年表にまとめてみましょう。

The History of Harajuku

　　Harajuku is known as a center of youth and fashion culture in Japan. However, it looked very different in the past. Before the Edo period, it was a small town on the Kamakura Highway and local people offered a place to stay to travelers. Farmers in this area engaged in agricultural work for a living. However, due to the poor quality of the land, the villages never really prospered. Through the late 19th century, many Japanese traditional umbrella artisans resided in the area. Later, Meiji Jingu Shrine was built in 1920, and the area became the main route to the shrine. In fact, it is only in the 1970s that Harajuku gained a nationwide reputation as a fashion mecca, especially among young people. Harajuku will probably become even better known internationally in the future.

時を表す語： _____

Time	Events / Details
Pre-Edo	

Grammar for Writing

[Tense] 時制／[Modal 1] 助動詞 1（will）

歴史の Time Order Paragraph を記述する際には時制を適切に用いましょう。

1. 過去形：既に起こった出来事について
   In ancient times, the Minoans **settled** in the south-western end of the island.　(Ex.A)

2. 現在形：現在の状態 / 現在を含む歴史について / 歴史的事実
   It **is** widely considered to be one of the most beautiful islands ～　(Ex.A)

3. 助動詞 will：未来の可能性・予定・展望について
   Harajuki **will** probably become even better known internationally ～　(Ex.B)

Exercise C

動詞を適切な形に直し（　　）内に入れ英文を完成させましょう。

1. "Paragraph" という言葉は、古代ギリシア語の「パラグラフォス」に由来します。(derive)
   The word "paragraph" (　　　　　) from the ancient Greek word *paragraphos*.

2. ベリーズはマヤ文明の貿易の中心だったと言われています。(be 動詞)
   It (　　　　) said that Belize (　　　　　) the trading center of the Maya Civilization.

3. 859 年に設立されたモロッコのカラウィーン大学は、現存する世界最古の高等教育機関と言われています。(found)
   Morocco's University of al-Qarawiyyin, (　　　　　) in 859 AD, is said to be the oldest existing higher education institution in the world.

4. ミラノは、ルネッサンス期と同様に 21 世紀もファッションの中心地の一つです。(be 動詞)
   Milan (　　　　) one of the fashion capitals of the 21st century just as it (　　　　) a center of fashion in the Renaissance era.

5. 2019 年夏、ミャンマーのバガン歴史地区がユネスコの世界遺産に登録されました。(add)
   In the summer of 2019, Bagan, a historical area in Myanmar, was (　　　　) to the UNESO's list of World Heritage sites.

Exercise D

和文を参考にし英単語を並べ替えましょう。なお、文頭にくる語も小文字で記してあります。

1. 今後50年で世界はどのようになるでしょうか。

[the / look / 50 / world / what / in / years / will / like/ next / the]?

2. 日本の人口は5年で100万人近く減少しました。

[years/ million / Japan's / by / people / in / population / fell / nearly / one / five].

3. 詩人のバイロン卿はかつて言いました。「最も優れた未来の予言者は過去なり。」

Lord Byron, a poet, once said, " [future / best / the / past / is / the / prophet / of / the]."

4. インドの多くの宗教における時間の概念は直線的ではなく円環的です。

[is / rathar / than / many / Indian / cyclical / in / concept / time / the / linear / of / religions].

Useful Vocabulary for the Topic

Exercise E

次の語句の意味を a. ～ j. の中から選びましょう。

_____ 1. dates back   a. 繁栄する

_____ 2. explorer   b. 統治する

_____ 3. emigrate   c. 開発者

_____ 4. settlement   d. 戦い

_____ 5. developer   e. 定住（地）・入植地

_____ 6. rise and fall   f. 革命

_____ 7. reign   g. 探検家

_____ 8. flourish   h. 遡る

_____ 9. battle   i. 移住する

_____ 10. revolution   j. 盛衰

Outline

まちの歴史を時系列に紹介する Paragraph の Outline を作成してみましょう。

Topic	
Supporting idea ①	
Supporting idea ②	
Supporting idea ③	
Conclusion	

Writing a paragraph

Outline をもとに Paragraph を書いてみましょう。各 Supporting Point に Detail を書き加えましょう。

UNIT 7 食べ物を分類してみよう（Classification）

アリストテレス以来、様々な分類方法が試みられてきました。生物学をはじめ、分類することは科学や研究の基本とも言えるでしょう。また、類型化は情報の整理にもつながるでしょう。

［本課の目標］
・ 食べ物の分類について考える。
・ Classification Paragraph
　構造・文法・語彙を理解する。（Input）
・ Outline/Paragrah を作成する。（Output）

Warm Up

クラスメイトにインタビューをしてみましょう。

1. What's your favorite food?

2. What did you have for breakfast this morning? / What did you have for dinner last night?

3. Do you eat any special food to stay healthy?

4. How often do you eat out?

【Expansion activity】

食べ物に関するトピックを1つ決め、小グループでディスカッションをしてみましょう。

ディスカッションには主に以下の2通りがあります。

① 意見・アイディア・経験等を共有するタイプ　　例）上記1〜4の質問
② 物事を決めるタイプ　　　　　　　　　　　例）最も健康的な日本食は何か。
　　　　　　　　　　　　　　　　　　　　　　　懇親会のお店はどこが良いか。

Paragraph Analysis

Classification

何かを分類する際に用いる Paragraph のパターンです。
① 基準を設定し（根拠）それに基づいて分類します。
② それぞれの類型について具体的に説明をします。
③ 結論として分類を要約します。

＜ Useful Expressions ＞

基準の設定： according to / based on / depending on

分類：	★	～ can / may be divided / grouped / classified / categorized into ～
	★	groups / types/ classifications / categories/ kinds / segments / varieties
	★	There are three types / groups/ kinds / classes of ～ / a variety of ～
	★	The first / second / third group consists of ～ / falls into / belongs to ～
	★	～ includes

Model Paragraph

Exercise A

次の Paragraph の分類の根拠を確認し、図に適切な情報を書き入れましょう。

Classification of Foods

All our foods can be divided into three groups according to the functions of nutrients. The first group is "energy producing foods", which include products rich in carbohydrates. Intake of these foods is important to maintain a sufficient energy level to carry out our daily activities. Foods such as rice, bread and potatoes are in this category. The second group "body building foods", which are rich in proteins, is necessary for the growth of our body cells. Fish, meat, and beans are in this category. The third group, rich in vitamins and minerals, is classified as "protective foods." It is essential for building our immune system. Vegetables, fruits and mushrooms fall into this category. In summary, the three groups of foods provide nutrients vital for keeping us healthy.

Topic Sentence: _____

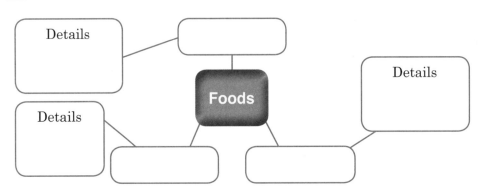

Concluding Sentence: _____

次の Paragraph を読み、分類方法及びそれに基づく 3 つのタイプを簡潔に記し、分類の表現を抜き出してみましょう。

Types of Rice

Rice is a staple food in many countries around the world. Varieties of rice may be classified into three types based on their characteristics. The first type, long-grain rice, is long and thin. It has a firm and dry texture. This type is typically used in Indian cuisine. Another type is medium-grain rice. This type of rice is often used in Middle Eastern and Spanish dishes, and it is also considered most appropriate for making creamy desserts. The third type, short-grain rice, is soft and tender. Most varieties of rice grown in Japan fall into this category. It is also the kind of rice best suited for making sushi. In conclusion, rice comes in many varieties but generally speaking, it can be grouped into these three categories.

Introductory Sentence: ....

分類方法： ....

1	・特徴 ・例
2	・特徴 ・例
3	・特徴 ・例

分類の表現： ....

［Modals 2］助動詞 2 (can, may)

分類の基準を示す際に、can や may の可能性を表す用法（できる、しうる）が一般的に用いられます。

1. All our foods **can** be divided into three groups according to the functions of nutrients. (Ex.A)
2. Varieties of rice **may** be classified into three types based on their characteristics. (Ex.B)

Exercise C

和文を参考にして適切な英単語を下の語群より選び（　　）内に入れましょう。

1. 食品産業にはどのようなものがありますか。
   What are the (　　　　　) of food industry?

2. 食品製造業は3つの型に分けることができます。
   The food manufacturing industry (　　　　　) be divided into three segments.

3. 会社は、所在地、規模、加工の仕方により分類することができます。
   Companies (　　　　　) be grouped according to location, scale and type of manufacturing.

4. この会社の主力商品には、清涼飲料やアルコール飲料が含まれます。
   This company's main products (　　　　　) soft drinks and alcoholic beverages.

5. 様々な種類の緑茶が現在は北米の多くのスーパーで入手可能です。健康に良いと認識されるようになったためです。
   A wide (　　　　　) of green tea is now available in many supermarkets in North America, as people recognize the heatlh benefits of this drink.

include	may	categories	variety	can

Exercise D

和文の意味に合うように英単語を並べ替えましょう。なお、文頭にくる語も小文字で記してあります。

1. 日本のラーメンの代表的な味には、塩、醤油、味噌、豚骨があります。

   [miso / salt / broth / typical / Japanese / and / soy sauce / tonkotsu / includes/ ramen].

2. (1) チーズの分類方法の一つにその硬さが挙げられます。

   [is / to / way / firmness /classify /to / one / cheese/ according / its].

   (2) クリームチーズは、フレッシュチーズの範疇に属します。

   [falls / cheese / category /cheese / fresh / into / cream].

3. 伝統的なペルー料理は、地理的条件により、海岸地帯、山岳地帯、熱帯雨林地域の3種類に分けることができます。

   [can / cuisine / location / on / varieties / divided / traditional / into / three / be / Peruvian / depending] : seaside, mountain and rainforest.

Useful Vocabulary for the Topic

Exercise E

次の語句の意味を a. ～ j. の中から選びましょう。

_____	1. gastronomy	a.	調味料
_____	2. organic food	b.	生の食材
_____	3. carbohydrate	c.	大豆製品
_____	4. raw food	d.	合成肉
_____	5. processed food	e.	遺伝子組み換え
_____	6. soy bean products	f.	調理法・美食学
_____	7. condiment	g.	ゲノム編集
_____	8. synthetic meat	h.	有機農産物
_____	9. GM (Genetic Modification)	i.	炭水化物
_____	10. genome editing	j.	加工食品

Outline

食べ物を選び、分類の基準を明確にし、各類型の特徴を踏まえて Outline を作成してみましょう。

Topic	
Supporting idea ①	
Supporting idea ②	
Supporting idea ③	
Conclusion	

Writing a paragraph

Outline をもとに Paragraph を書いてみましょう。各 Supporting Point に Detail を書き加えましょう。

UNIT 8

二つの国の類似点と相違点について考えてみよう
（Comparison & Contrast）

　ある物事や人を描写する際、他との類似点を挙げて比較したり、相違点を挙げて対比すると、より一層その物事や人の特性が明確でわかり易くなります。

［本課の目標］
・ 二つの国・地域の類似点と相違点について考える。
・ Comparison & Contrast Paragraph
　構造・語彙・文法を理解する。（Input）
・ Outline/Paragrah を作成する。（Output）

Warm Up

A. 日本以外の国や地域を一つ選び、日本との類似点（similarities）や相違点（differences）について自分なりに考え、下の表に書き込んでみましょう。

Similarities
・（例）Both Japan and the U.S. are democratic countries.
・
・
・
・
Differences
・（例）Japan is a small country while the U.S. has a large territory.
・
・
・
・

B. 自分が挙げた similarities と differences について互いに紹介し、意見を交換しましょう。

Paragraph Analysis

Comparison and Contrast

　Comparison（比較）の Paragraph では、二つの異なる事柄について複数の類似点や共通点について論じます。contrast（対比）の Paragraph では相違点について論じます。

＜ Useful Expressions ＞

Comparison の Paragraph で用いられる表現には以下のようなものがあります。

　　A is similar to B. / Both A and B are _____. / A is _____, and so is B. /
　　A is as _____ as B.
　　・Japanese and Korean languages are pretty similar.
　　・Both Japanese and Korean use words derived from Chinese.

Contrast の Paragraph で用いられる表現には以下のようなものがあります。

　　on the other hand / on the contrary / unlike~ / while~ / although~ / nevertheless /
　　however / A and B are different in the following ways:
　　・There are important differences in the way Japanese and Americans communicate.
　　・Communication styles can differ depending on the culture of the country.

Model Paragraph

Exercise A

次の Comparison の Paragraph を読み、構成について考えましょう。

Similarities of Japanese and Korean Languages

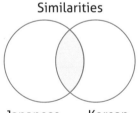

　It is interesting that once Japanese teenagers start learning Korean, they will make progress in it faster than in English since Japanese and Korean are pretty similar. First, the word order is mostly the same. For example, if you say, "I made a phone call to a friend yesterday," the word order in Korean and Japanese would be as follows: "I / yesterday / a friend / a phone call / made." Second, vocabulary can be quite similar too. Both Japanese and Korean use words derived from Chinese, and both languages borrow heavily from English. Third, expressions of politeness play an important role in both Korean and Japanese. These expressions illustrate the role of the Confucianist philosophy in the cultures of the two countries. Although there are obviously many differences between the two languages, Korean is similar to Japanese in many ways.

Topic Sentence の主張

```
[                                                                              ]
```

Supporting Sentence 1 で挙げられている類似点①

Detail 1（類似点①の具体例）

Supporting Sentence 2 で挙げられている類似点②

Detail 2（類似点②の詳細）

Supporting Sentence 3 で挙げられている類似点③

Detail 3（類似点③の詳細）

Concluding Sentence（主題の確認とまとめ）

Exercise B

次の Contrast の Paragraph を読み、①～⑥に入る語（句）を各々の選択肢から選び、Paragraph を完成させましょう。

　　Communication styles can differ depending on the culture of the country. [①], there are important differences in the way Japanese and Americans communicate. In Japan people generally do not show their feelings openly. [②], in the United States you are expected to express yourself clearly since American society is very diverse. Japanese society [③] tends to be more hierarchical. People use many levels of politeness depending on the age, gender and the status of the person in front of them. [④], when making a decision the Japanese prefer to work in a group, reaching a consensus though discussion. [⑤], in America decisions are often made by the person with the most authority. Being aware of differences in communication styles is very important [⑥] you do business overseas or simply travel to another country.

---

① By the way, Thus, Although, Nevertheless, But
② Likely, While, In the same way, Because, On the contrary
③ also, and, again, that, for
④ In case, Furthermore, From then on, To repeat, To sum up
⑤ To conclude, For instance, Likewise, On the other hand, Furthermore
⑥ even if, wherever, whether, though, despite

［Modals 3］助動詞3（would, could, might）

would, could, might とは：過去のほか、丁寧表現や低い可能性を表す助動詞

would, could, might の文構造：主語 ＋ would/could/might ＋ 動詞の原型

1. would（過去の習慣・強い意志、丁寧な依頼）
   We would stay up and talk when she visited me.（よく～したものだ）
   She wouldn't apologize for her mistake.（どうしても～しようとしなかった）
   Would you please send me the missing information?（～して頂けませんか）

2. could（能力、可能性、丁寧な依頼）
   I could run just as fast as you do when I was young.（～できた）
   Even a war could break out under such circumstances.（ひょっとして～する可能性もある）
   Could I ask you a favor?（～しても宜しいでしょうか）

3. might（推量）
   It might be too easy for you.（ひょっとして～かもしれない）

Exercise C

次の各文を読み、文脈に最も合う助動詞を選びましょう。

1. I (might / would / could) appreciate it if you could reply ASAP.
2. How (might / would / could) you know what I was going to do?
3. (Might / Would / Could) you mind opening the window?
4. Any restaurant (might / would / could) be fine with me as long as it's not too expensive.
5. He (might / would / could) well be planning his revenge.

Exercise D

かっこの中の語句を並べ替えて文を完成させましょう。

1. I [staying / grandparents / with / might / my / be] this summer.
2. [it / could / English / you / into / translate], please?
3. He [to / open / might / your ideas / more / be] if you explained them in writing.
4. If you had asked me, [better / could / it / do / I].
5. The professor asked [might / student / help / the / she / if] him.

Useful Vocabulary for the Topic

Exercise E

次の語句の意味を a. 〜 j. の中から選びましょう。

_____ 1. staple food a. 諺
_____ 2. monarchy b. 地形
_____ 3. democratic c. 特産品
_____ 4. work ethic d. 主食
_____ 5. values e. 民族的背景
_____ 6. proverb f. 民主主義の
_____ 7. topography g. 国民性
_____ 8. national trait h. 労働観
_____ 9. ethnicity i. 君主制
_____ 10. local specialty j. 価値観

Outline

二つの異なる国を比較／対比する Paragraph の Outline を作りましょう。それぞれの言語、生活習慣、価値観、コミュニケーション・スタイルなどを調べて例示しましょう。

Topic	
Supporting idea ①	
Supporting idea ②	
Supporting idea ③	
Conclusion	

Writing a Paragraph

OutlineをもとにParagraphを書いてみましょう。各Supporting SentenceにDetailを書き加えましょう。

UNIT 9 社会の変化について書いてみよう（Cause & Effect）

　あるできごとの原因（cause）と結果（effect）の因果関係を説明する場合、まず結果として表れている事象を明らかにした上で、その原因・理由を具体的に挙げていきます。

［本課の目標］
- 社会の変化について考える。
- Cause and Effect Paragraph
  構造・文法・語彙を理解する。（Input）
- Outline/Paragraph を作成する。（Output）

Warm Up

A. 次の質問に答えましょう。

1. What social issue are you mostly interested in?

2. Why are they important? (give 1-2 reasons)

3. What are the main causes of these social issues?

4. How do you get information about this topic?

5. How do you think these changes will affect society in the future?

B. Aの質問についてパートナーと相互にインタビューをして、意見交換しましょう。

Cause and Effect

　因果関係を説明する際には、まず Topic Sentence で結果として表れている事象を紹介し、Supporting Sentences で具体的な原因・理由を明らかにします。結果の事象と結びつきの強い原因・理由を具体的に複数挙げることで、説得力のある論理展開をすることができます。

＜ Useful Expressions ＞

「原因」を述べる時の表現には以下のようなものがあります。

　There are some major causes of…. / There are several reasons why…. / / because of… / due to… / thanks to… / owing to… / on account of…

　· Cavities（結果）can result from eating sweets（原因）.
　· *The first cause is* the spread of credit cards and electronic money.
　· *The next factor which* contributes to longevity *is the* healthy diet of most Japanese.

「結果」を述べる時の表現には以下のようなものがあります。

　therefore / so that… / thus / as a result / consequently / in the end / finally

　· Her plan ended in failure（結果）.
　· *This has led to* many important improvements in health.

Model Paragraph

Exercise A

次の Paragraph を読み、3 つの原因と、その結果として表れている事象を図の中に書き入れましょう。

　Nowadays more than ninety percent of all payments is cashless in Korea, and nearly 70% percent in the U.K. Cashless payments are getting increasingly common worldwide. The first cause is the spread of credit cards. In Europe even very small payments can be made with a credit card. Cashless payments are also encouraged by governments. It is a very efficient way to collect data about consumer behavior. This leads to new business opportunities. Another benefit of cashless payment is that it can actually reduce crime. As cash is being used less, robberies become less frequent. In the future, our society may become even less dependent on cash, and we will rarely get to see paper money. There are many benefits of cashless payments and both consumers and businesses will certainly appreciate the convenience of this new style of transactions.

Causes		Effect
1	→	
2	→	
3	→	

次の各文を読み、Introductory Sentence に続いて、Topic Sentence から Detail Sentence ③まで、正しい順序に並べ替えましょう。最後の一文は Concluding Sentence です。

The average life expectancy of the Japanese in 2017 was among the highest in the world. (Introductory Sentence)

① The traditional Japanese cuisine is low in fat and is nutritious.
② Quality of life is a key factor as well.
③ This has led to many important improvements in health.
④ The next factor is the healthy diet of most Japanese.
⑤ First of all, advanced medical treatment is available to all residents of Japan thanks to national health insurance.
⑥ In Japan, the gap between the rich and the poor is relatively small. Unemployment and crime rates are also quite low.
⑦ Three possible causes of this phenomenon could be national health coverage, the healthy Japanese diet, and a high quality of life.

There are probably other factors but in my view, these three reasons are the most important. (Concluding Sentence)

(   ) ➡ (   ) ➡ (   ) ➡ (   ) ➡ (   ) ➡ (   ) ➡ (   )

Grammar for Writing

[Coordinating Conjunctions] 等位接続詞

従位接続詞は主節に従位節を結び付けますが、等位接続詞は対等な関係にある語・句・節を結び付け、and（連結）、but（対立）、or（選択）、so（結果）などがあります。

Come **and** see me anytime.（連結）
She saw what happened there with her own eyes, **yet** she just couldn't believe it.（対立）
To be, **or** not to be; that is the question.（選択）
I felt sick, **so** decided to skip my afternoon classes and go home.（結果）

Exercise C

文脈に合った接続詞を選択肢から選びましょう。

1. For here, (   ) to go?
2. He got into all the top colleges, (   ) he must be pretty smart.
3. I've never been to Paris, (   ) I would love to go there one of these days.
4. Hurry up, (   ) you'll miss the bus.
5. Turn right at the next light, (   ) you will find the store at the end of the street.

and	but	or	so

Exercise D

かっこの中の語句を並べ替えて文を完成させましょう。

1. My mother [our / dried / washed / and / clothes] them.

2. Either [has / your / do / you / or / to / sister] this.

3. Not that I hate [time / I / but / have / studying / don't] to study.

4. I had been sick for a while, [really / schedule / I / so / behind / was].

5. I [and / straight / was / went / exhausted] to bed after getting home.

Useful Vocabulary for the Topic

Exercise E

次の語句の意味を a. 〜 j. の中から選びましょう。

_____ 1. gender gap index   a. 移民政策

_____ 2. birthrate   b. 格差

_____ 3. organ transplant   c. 多国籍企業

_____ 4. immigration policy   d. 仮想通貨

_____ 5. aging society   e. 男女格差指数

_____ 6. multinational corporation   f. 持続可能な開発

_____ 7. disparity   g. 高齢化社会

_____ 8. virtual currency   h. 人工知能

_____ 9. sustainable development   i. 臓器移植

_____ 10. artificial intelligence   j. 出生率

Outline

身の回りの社会の変化について、その原因と結果を論じる Paragraph の Outline を作りましょう。その変化の主な 3 つの原因を例示しましょう。

Topic	
Supporting idea ①	
Supporting idea ②	
Supporting idea ③	
Conclusion	

Writing a Paragraph

OutlineをもとにParagraphを書いてみましょう。各Supporting SentenceにDetailを書き加えましょう。

UNIT 10 社会課題の解決策を考えてみよう（Problem-Solution）

　社会には様々な課題がありますが、その原因究明に加え解決方法を探ることは、より良い社会の実現につながるでしょう。

［本課の目標］
・ 社会課題について考える。
・ Problem-Solution Paragraph
　 構造・語彙・文法を理解する。（Input）
・ Outline/Paragrah を作成する。（Output）

Warm Up

1. これまでのあなたの人生に起こった問題について、どのように自分なりに解決したかを思い出してみましょう。

2. 社会課題や解決法をブレーンストーミングしクラスメイトと共有してみましょう。

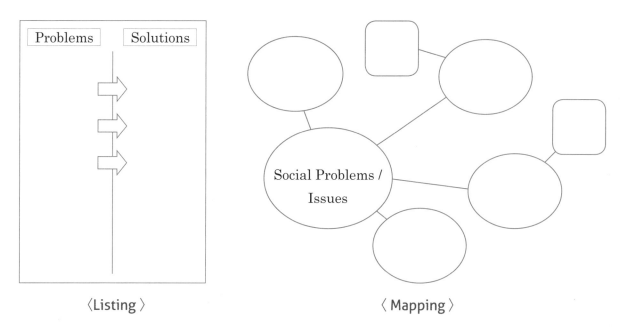

〈Listing〉　　　　　　　　　　　　　〈Mapping〉

【Expansion activity】
〈Verbal〉小グループで声に出してブレーンストーミングしてみましょう。

Paragraph Analysis

Problem –Solution

課題の解決策を示す際に用いられる Paragraph のパターンです。

① まず何が課題なのかを明確にします。

② 次にその解決策を順次提示し、具体例などを含めより詳しく説明をします。

③ 結論として全体の要点をまとめます。

＜ Useful Expressions ＞

[課題の提起]　～ is a problem, but a possible solution is ～
[解決策の提示]　～ is a possible way of solving the problem

One way of solving the problem is ～ / possible (effective) solution is ～

One idea is ～ / another solution is ～ / Finally

_____ will / may / might / could solve the problem / tackle the problem

Model Paragraph

Exercise A

次の Paragraph の構造を確認し枠内を埋めましょう。

Solutions to Overcrowded Trains

　Crowded trains are a cause of stress for people living in cities, but there are several solutions to this problem. One idea is to set up different working hours for companies located in the same area. For example, some companies may start work at 8:30am while at others it can begin at 9:00 or even 9:30. Obviously, the end of the working day would no longer be the same for all businesses either. Another solution is to allow employees to work from home once or twice a week. This way the number of passengers on trains will definitely decrease. Finally, developing double-decker trains will increase capacity and allow each train to carry more passengers. As you can see, by thinking creatively and implementing innovative policies, we can make the train commute more comfortable for passengers.

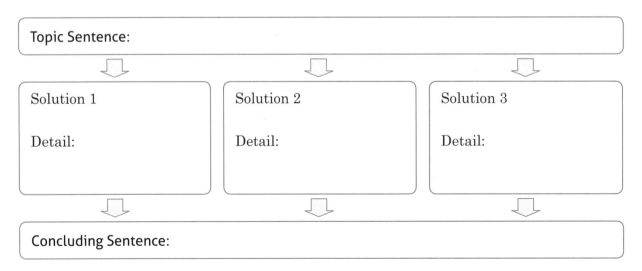

Topic Sentence:

Solution 1

Detail:

Solution 2

Detail:

Solution 3

Detail:

Concluding Sentence:

次の Paragraph の Main Idea 及び具体例を 2 つ記してみましょう。

Inventive Solutions

Until recently, life for residents of rural or remote areas was inconvenient, especially in terms of access to education and medical services. However, thanks to the development of online technologies, the situation has improved remarkably. Today, once we are connected to the Internet, we can register for a wide variety of university-level courses. Many of them are offered for free by a growing number of top colleges. It has become possible to obtain a qualification online. Therefore, it is no longer necessary to move. Medical services have also become much more accessible. Using sophisticated computer networks doctors can observe their patients remotely, recommend a treatment and offer consultations. These are examples of how the technology can help bring communities closer and make it possible for people everywhere to lead more comfortable and fulfilling lives.

Main Idea:

Example 1

Details

Example 2

Details

Subordinating Conjunctions ［従位接続詞］

従属節（名詞節・形容詞節・副詞節）を導く接続詞です。

Problem-Solution 型の Paragraph にも用途に応じ従位接続詞が用いられます。

＜時＞	before / after / until / till / as soon as / whenever / while / by the time
＜場所＞	where / wherever
＜理由＞	as / because / so that / since / why
＜条件＞	once / if / unless / even if / in case / providing / considering
＜譲歩＞	although / even though / whereas / whether or not
＜比較＞	than / rather than
＜制限・範囲＞	as long as / as far as

【例】

1. **As** you can see, by thinking creatively and implementing innovative... (Ex. A)

2. **Once** we are connected to the Internet, we can.... (Ex.B)

Exercise C

和文を参考にし（　　　）内に適切な語を下の語群より選びましょう。

1. 健康で長生きするために、良く食べ良く寝て定期的に体を動かしましょう。
   Eat well, sleep well, and exercise regularly (　　　　　　　) you can live a healthy and long life.

2. 地震センサーが僅かな振動でも感知するとブザーが鳴り始めます。
   (　　　　　　　) an earthquake sensor detects even a minor tremor, it will buzz.

3. クリーンエネルギーへの関心は高まってはいるものの化石燃料は未だ広く使用されています。
   (　　　　　　　) there is a growing interest in clean energy, fossil fuels are still being used widely.

4. その会社は、全従業員の残業代を増やすと発表しました。
   The company announced (　　　　　　　) it would increase overtime pay for all employees.

5. 世界には多くの飢えている人々がいる一方で食べ物を無駄にしている人々もいます。
   There are many people suffering from hunger, (　　　　　　　) many people waste food around the world.

that	even though	while	so that	whenever	than	in case

Exercise D

和文の意味に照らして英単語を並べ替えましょう。なお、文頭にくる語も小文字で記してあります。

1. 私の地元は小さな町ですが沢山の文化的な魅力があります。
   [many / although / is / small / attractions / my / it / has / hometown / cultural].

2. 従来のレジ袋ではなくエコバックを使う人が増えています。
   [the / bags /more / old-fashioned / rather /plastic / using/ people / eco-friendly / than / are / bags].

3. 最後に出る人は必ず電気を消すようにすべきです。
   [to / turn / make / leave / the / is / should / the / to / off / whoever / lights / sure / last].

4. 問題は、あなたが問題だと思わない限り問題にはなりませんよ。
   [is / problem / an / not / issue / a / unless /it / think / become / problem / does / you / a].

Useful Vocabulary for the Topic

Exercise E

次の語句の意味を a. ～ j. の中から選びましょう。

_____	1. well-being	a.	資源
_____	2. disaster prevention	b.	人権
_____	3. child poverty	c.	社会保障
_____	4. cultural inheritance	d.	取り組む
_____	5. labor shortage	e.	防災
_____	6. diversity	f.	子どもの貧困
_____	7. human rights	g.	文化継承
_____	8. resources	h.	多様性
_____	9. tackle	i.	労働力不足
_____	10. social security	j.	身体的・社会的・精神的に良好

Outline

社会課題を 1 つ選び、解決策を含めた Outline を作成してみましょう。

My topic	
Supporting idea ①	
Supporting idea ②	
Supporting idea ③	
Conclusion	

Writing a paragraph

Outline をもとに Paragraph を書いてみましょう。各 Supporting Point に Detail を書き加えましょう。

UNIT 11　Paragraph から Presentation へ 1 （Introduction）

　Presentation のもととなる概念は、アリストテレスの『弁論術』、日本の巻物形式の『勧進帳』を用いた勧進や紙芝居などにもみることができます。Part III では、英語による一般的な Presentation の基本構造や視覚資料について学びます。

Presentation 全体の構成

　以下の図が、わかりやすい Presentation のための基本構造です。これまでに学んできた Paragraph の基本構造と似ていることを確かめましょう。

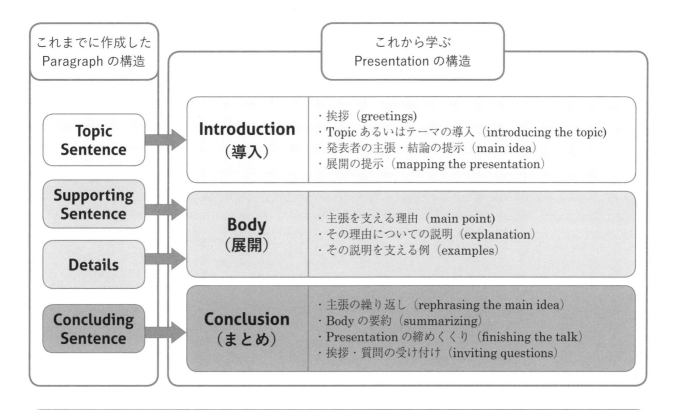

これまでに作成した Paragraph の構造	これから学ぶ Presentation の構造	
Topic Sentence	**Introduction** （導入）	・挨拶 （greetings） ・Topic あるいはテーマの導入 （introducing the topic） ・発表者の主張・結論の提示 （main idea） ・展開の提示 （mapping the presentation）
Supporting Sentence **Details**	**Body** （展開）	・主張を支える理由 （main point） ・その理由についての説明 （explanation） ・その説明を支える例 （examples）
Concluding Sentence	**Conclusion** （まとめ）	・主張の繰り返し （rephrasing the main idea） ・Body の要約 （summarizing） ・Presentation の締めくくり （finishing the talk） ・挨拶・質問の受け付け （inviting questions）

> **Presentation の基本構造の役割とは？**
>
> 　わかりやすい Presentation をするために大切なことは何でしょうか。声の大きさや提示資料などももちろん大切ですが、それ以前に発表者と聴衆の双方が Presentation の基本構造の理解を共有していることが重要です。また、基本構造に則って発表することは、発表者が考えたことを効率よく聴衆に伝えるうえでも役立ちます。

Part III

Good morning, everyone. I'm happy to have an opportunity to talk to you here today. Let me ask you a question. How many of you ride a train in the morning? Raise your hand. I see. And how many among you have to stand on the train because it is really crowded? Ah, almost everyone. Today I would like to suggest some solutions to overcrowded trains. According to a government report, during rush hour, trains in and around the capital are filled to 165% capacity on average, and some lines run at almost double their capacity. Crowded trains are definitely a cause of stress for people in cities, however, there are several ways to make the situation better. In this presentation, I would like to focus on three solutions to this problem: staggered working hours, work from home, and double decker trains.

My first idea is expanding staggered working hours. This means setting up different working hours for companies located in the same area. For example, some companies' work may start at 8:30a.m., while at others it can begin at 9:00 or even 9:30. Obviously, the end of the working day would no longer be the same for all businesses either. As part of this plan, some companies are already allowing their employees flexible working hours. One company actually offers 13 variations of working hours. Several companies have tried flexible working hours on a trial basis and found out that the employees' commute had become more comfortable, their work efficiency had improved and the quality of their private lives had also improved.

Another solution is to allow employees to work from home once or twice a week. This way, the number of passengers on trains will decrease. In addition, some people could live and work in a rural area and communicate with the office remotely. Actually, some towns and villages around Japan are inviting people to move there from urban areas, so that they can revitalize local economies. People can enjoy a more relaxed lifestyle in the countryside with no need to use public transit, but still stay connected to their workplace in the city.

Finally, introducing double-decker trains will increase passenger capacity. Double-decker trains can accommodate over 50% more passengers, so it will obviously be a promising development. In the future, it may be possible to run double-decker trains equipped with doors on both levels by building two-story platforms so that the passengers can get on and off trains smoothly.

In conclusion, by thinking creatively and implementing innovative policies, we can make the train commute more comfortable for passengers and also improve the quality of life in the cities. Obviously, this is a major problem for millions of residents. We looked at three possible solutions today for the crowded trains: staggered working hours, work from home, and double-decker trains. In order to come up with a realistic solution we all need to think "outside the box."
Now we still have some time left, so please feel free to ask any questions.

Introduction の構成

　導入では、その後の Presentation 全体を聞くために必要な情報を提示します。ここの出来栄えで、Presentation 全体で自分が言いたいことが伝わるかが決まります。Introduction の構成要素としては以下のようなものがあります。

1. 挨拶（greetings）

　まずは発表者と聴衆との信頼関係を築くことが重要です。時間帯や立場を踏まえたことばを適切に選択しましょう。その際に、一般的な挨拶にとどまらず聴衆への質問や挙手をさせて参加意識を高める方法なども用いられます。

例）Good morning, everyone. I'm happy to have an opportunity to talk to you here today. Let me ask you a question. How many of you ride a train in the morning? Raise your hand. I see. And how many among you have to stand on the train because it is really crowded? Ah, almost everyone.

2. Topic の導入（introducing the topic）

　次に説明する「発表者の主張」を効果的に聴衆に伝えるためにも、これから何について話すかをあらかじめ提示します。

例）Today I would like to suggest some solutions to overcrowded trains. According to a government report, during rush hour, trains in and around the capital are filled to 165% capacity on average, and some lines run at almost double their capacity.

3. 発表者の主張・まとめの提示（main idea）

　発表を通して最も言いたいことを述べます。これまでの Unit で作成した Topic Sentence を一部変形させることで Presentation 用の原稿を作成します。

例）Crowded trains are definitely a cause of stress for people in cities, however, there are several ways to make the situation better.

4. 展開の提示（outline）

　Presentation の構成を簡単にまとめます。聴衆は「これから Presentation がどのような順番で進んでいくのか」を知り、内容を把握しやすくなります。

例）In this presentation, I would like to focus on three solutions to this problem: staggered working hours, work from home, and double decker trains.
　　　　　　　①　　　　　　　　　　②　　　　　　　　　③

Language for Presentation

Presentation の Introduction で使える表現としては、以下のようなものがあります。

1. 挨拶

    Hello, everyone.

    Good morning / Good afternoon, ladies and gentlemen.

    I'm happy to have an opportunity to make this presentation here today.

2. **Topic** の導入

    Today, I'd like to talk about (Topic).

    Today I'd like to suggest (Topic)

    My presentation today is about (Topic).

    The subject of this presentation is (Topic).

3. 発表者の主張・発表の目的

    Topic sentence

    The most important point of my presentation is (Topic Sentence).

4. 展開の提示

    In this presentation, I'd like to focus on ...

    In my brief presentation, I will outline three possible factors of ...

    My talk is divided into three parts.

    My speech will cover two areas.

Vocabulary for Presentation

Exercise

次の語句の意味を a. 〜 j. の中から選びましょう。

_____	1. focus	a.	主張する
_____	2. divide	b.	構成
_____	3. compose	c.	部分
_____	4. element	d.	挨拶
_____	5. opportunity	e.	機会
_____	6. subject	f.	主題
_____	7. greeting	g.	要素
_____	8. part	h.	構成する
_____	9. structure	i.	分ける
_____	10. argue	j.	焦点

Unit 10 で作成した Paragraph の主題文をもとに Introduction の原稿を完成させましょう。

1. 挨拶： ....

2. Topic の導入： ....

3. 発表者の主張： ....

....

4. 展開の提示： ....

....

Part III

Grammar for Presentation

［Nouns and Adjectives］名詞および形容詞

名詞（Nouns）

　普通名詞 − すべて可算名詞

　　Apples are fruits.　　An apple is a fruit.

　　The apple is a fruit.　　I like apples.

　固有名詞、集合名詞、物質名詞、抽象名詞

　　Her audience was all quiet.

　　There are three sheets of paper.

形容詞（Adjectives）

　Create beautiful and impactful slides for your presentation.

　He will be introduced by the previous speaker.

Visual aids

　効果的な Presentation を目指すうえで、内容がよく整理されていて言語面でも洗練されたものであることが大切なのは言うまでもありませんが、視覚的な提示資料を用いることで聴衆への意味伝達がスムーズになる場合があります。

　視覚資料の作成には、大学生にもおなじみの Microsoft 社の Power Point や Google Slides のほかにも、Keynote, Prezi など、たくさんのソフトウェアを利用することができます。自分に合ったソフトウェアを見つけて、より良い視覚資料の作成に取り組んでみましょう。本書では、特定のソフトウェアは想定せず、紙芝居の形式で一枚の紙をどのように構成するかを学んでいきます。

Introduction で用いられるスライド例

　Introduction でしばしば用いられるスライドには以下の 3 種類があります。

1. Title・氏名・日付：Title では文頭と 4 文字以上の単語は大文字で始めましょう
2. 主張：シンプルな表現で大きな文字で書きましょう
3. 構成：箇条書きと適切な字下げで Presentation 全体の構成を表現しましょう

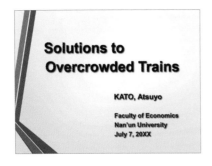 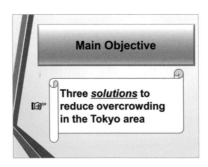 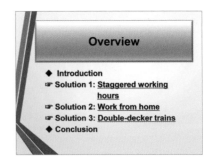

✓ TIPS

◆ 英語の発表に向けた提示資料作りの 8 つのポイント

・半角と全角の違いに注意する（全角は用いない）。
・Arial や Helvetica などサンセリフ体に属するフォントを用いる。
・文字サイズは統一する。
・文字の色は、基本の色以外には多くても強調するための 2 色程度にとどめる。
・アニメーションを用いる場合は最小限にする。
・1 枚のスライドには言いたいことを 1 つまでに抑える。
・原稿をそのまま貼り付けず、キーワードだけのシンプルな表現を用いる。
・文字よりも数字や図やグラフを重視する。

Paragraph から Presentation へ 2（Body）

Unit 11 では、Presentation 全体の基本構造と導入の作り方を学びました。Unit 12 で扱う Body は、文量が多くなりますが似た作業も多いので、コツをつかめばすぐに上達するでしょう。

Part III

Body（展開）の構成

　Body は、Introduction で述べた発表者の主張に対して、そう考えるに至った理由を論理的に述べる部分です。Part II では、1 つの段落内に Supporting Sentences と Details の組み合わせを3 つ作りました。その 3 つに対応させる形で、項目①、項目②、項目③の 3 つの部分から成る Body を作り主張を支持する形式を学びます。それぞれの Body に含めるべき要素には以下のようなものがあります。

1. 主張を支える理由（point）

　これまでに作ってきた支持文を用います。最初の理由を挙げる前に、これから Body が始まることを述べましょう。また、各項目の間には必ず転換語を用いましょう。

2. 明確に説明しきれなかった部分の補足説明（explanation）

　1 ではできるだけシンプルに要点を伝えるように心がけ、2 では足りない部分を補って理由が適切であることを説明しましょう。抽象的な事柄や前提知識が必要な部分は特に補足が必要です。これまでに作ってきた Detail がこれにあたる場合には、それを活用しましょう。

3. その理由を支える具体例や根拠となる情報（evidence）

　例を表す表現を用いて、それが具体例であることを聴衆に伝えましょう。これまでに作ってきた Detail がこれにあたる場合には、それを活用しましょう。

以下の（　　）から始まる文が Body の構成のどの要素かを語群より選び書き入れましょう。

explanation	point	evidence

■ 項目①

（　1　）**My first idea** is expanding staggered working hours. This means setting up different working hours for companies located in the same area.

（　2　）**For example**, some companies' work may start at 8:30a.m. while at others it can begin at 9:00 or even 9:30. Obviously, the end of the working day would no longer be the same for all businesses either.

（　3　）As part of this plan, <u>some companies are already allowing</u> their employees flexible working hours. <u>One company actually offers 13 variations of working hours.</u> <u>Several companies have tried flexible working hours</u> on a trial basis and found out that the employees' commute had become more comfortable, their work efficiency had improved and the quality of their private lives had also improved.

■ 項目②

（　1　）**Another solution** is to allow employees to work from home once or twice a week. This way, the number of passengers on trains will decrease.

（　2　）**In addition**, some people could live and work in a rural area and communicate with the office remotely.

（　3　）Actually, <u>some towns and villages around Japan are inviting people</u> to move there from urban areas, so that they can revitalize local economies. People can enjoy a more relaxed lifestyle in the countryside with no need to use public transit, but still stay connected to their workplace in the city.

■ 項目③

（　1　）**Finally**, introducing double-decker trains will increase passenger capacity.

（　2　）Double-decker trains <u>can accommodate over 50% more passengers</u>, so it will obviously be a promising development. In the future, it may be possible to run double-decker trains equipped with doors on both levels by building two-story platforms, so that the passengers can get on and off trains smoothly.

Language for Presentation

Presentation の Body で使える表現としては、他に以下のようなものもあります。

1. 主張を支える理由

First of all, I would like to tell you that S + V.

Another way to solve the problem is to (solutions).

I'm going to give you the final reason: S + V.

2. その理由についての説明

It includes (elements).

I would like to emphasize that S + V.

It should be noted that S + V.

3. その理由を支える具体例や根拠となる情報

According to media reports, S + V.

As was pointed out by X, S + V.　　As X points out, S + V.

For example, S + V.　　For instance, S + V.

Vocabulary for Presentation

Exercise B

次の語句の意味を a. ～ j. の中から選びましょう。

_____　 1. emphasis
_____　 2. note (verb)
_____　 3. stress (verb)
_____　 4. include
_____　 5. according to ～
_____　 6. point out
_____　 7. indicate
_____　 8. media report
_____　 9. academic studies
_____　10. case

a. 学術研究
b. ～によると
c. 指摘する
d. マスコミ報道
e. 事例
f. 注意を払う
g. 示す
h. 強調
i. 含む
j. 強調する

Your Own Presentation

Unit 10 で作成した Paragraph の Supporting Sentences と Detail を用いて Body の原稿を完成させましょう。

主張を支える理由①：

その理由についての説明①：

その理由を支える具体例①：

主張を支える理由②：

その理由についての説明②：

その理由を支える具体例②：

主張を支える理由③：

その理由についての説明③：

その理由を支える具体例③：

Grammar for Presentation

［Adverbs］副詞

副詞は、動詞だけでなく形容詞や他の副詞、文全体も修飾する場合がある。

1. 動詞を修飾する副詞 − 位置の自由度が高い
   Suddenly we realized the data was wrong.
   I usually prepare my presentation before class.
   Her presentation was delivered successfully.

2. 形容詞や他の副詞を修飾する副詞 − 原則として被修飾語の近く

His suggestion is very interesting.

They are practicing pretty hard.

The screen was large enough.

3. 文を修飾する副詞

Basically, my presentation was like an essay with an introduction, a body and a conclusion.

Fortunately, there is a variety of online tools to help you with your presentation.

Exercise C

次のそれぞれの文の誤りを指摘しましょう。

1. They don't remember the incident very good.

2. You must have heard its name ago.

3. This is so effective solution to the problem of school bullying.

4. The probability of getting the disease was very higher at the time.

5. Unfortunate, it was too late when I got the information.

Exercise D

(　　) 内の単語を用いて和文を英文にしましょう。

1. 速やかに保険会社に事故の状況を知らせましょう。(immediately / insurance company)

2. 労働者の権利は大いに尊重されなければなりません。(rights / at all time / respect)

3. 確実に、戦争で国際紛争を解決することはできないのです。
(certainly / international conflicts / war)

4. 規則正しい睡眠をとることは実際には簡単です。(actually / easy / regular sleeping hours)

　Body は文量が多いので、以下で学ぶポイントに注意したうえで多角的に情報を盛り込み、冗長な発表にならないように工夫しましょう。発表者が自分の意見を説得的に伝えるための工夫としては、根拠を明確に示すことが大切です。つまり、自分の思い込みや直感にもとづく議論ではなく、主張に至る判断材料がありそれを聴衆に示すということが求められます。それには、以下の注意点があります。

Body で用いられるスライド例

　Body でしばしば用いられるスライドには以下の 3 種類があります。

1. 主張を支える理由：理由が複数ある場合は適切な連番をつけシンプルな表現で書きましょう
2. その理由についての説明：必要に応じて理由に補足説明をしましょう
3. その理由を支える具体例：図表やイラストを用いながら具体例を示しましょう

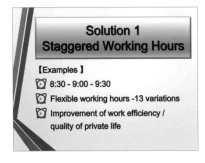 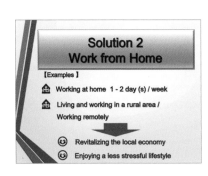 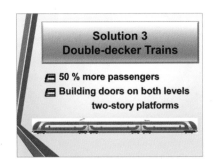

☑ TIPS

◆ 英語の発表に向けた情報倫理の 8 つのポイント

　Body などで具体例や根拠となる情報を示す際には、著作権法をはじめ守るべきルールがあります。

・キャラクターや他人の肖像などを無許可で掲載しない。
・引用した場合にはタイトルや URL 等の出典情報を示す。
・引用した情報には勝手な改訂を加えない。
・聞いた話等ではなく、新聞・雑誌や公的機関の発行物等の公共性の高い情報源を用いる。
・間接的な引用は控え、可能な限り原典にあたる。
・SNS や個人ブログ等の引用は控え、情報源とする際にも根拠をしっかりと確かめる。
・可能な限り複数の情報源を参照する。
・人や団体を誹謗中傷する内容は掲載しない。

Paragraph から Presentation へ 3（Conclusion）

Unit 11, Unit 12 では、Unit 10 で作った Paragraph を
もとに Presentation の Introduction と Body の作り方を
学びました。Unit 13 では、同様に Presentation の締めく
くりである Conclusion（まとめ）の基本構造を学びます。

Conclusion の構成

Conclusion は、Introduction と Body で述べた内容を短くまとめながら、発表者の主張を再度
明確に述べます。主張に対する根拠を既に聴衆と共有していることで、発表者の主張はより聴衆に
伝わりやすくなるでしょう。Part 2 で作成した Concluding Sentence の文をもとにして主張を繰
り返し、さらに Body でも用いた 3 つの Supporting Sentences 支持文に言及する形式を学びます。
Conclusion に含めるべき要素には以下のようなものがあります。

1. 主張の繰り返し（**rephrasing the main idea**）

　これまでに作った Paragraph の Concluding Sentence を用います。主題文と全く同じ文章に
ならないよう、別の角度から同じ内容の主張を述べましょう。また、必ず転換語から始めましょう。

例）In conclusion, by thinking creatively and implementing innovative policies, we can
make the train commute more comfortable for passengers and also improve the
quality of life in the cities.

2. Body の要約（**summarizing**）

　Body で触れた 3 つの Supporting Sentences を 1 文程度で簡単に触れましょう。Body で述
べたことの確認に過ぎませんので、シンプルな表現を心がけましょう。

例）We looked at three possible solutions today for the crowded trains: staggered working
hours, working from home, and double-decker trains.

3. Presentation の締めくくり（**finishing the talk**）

　提言、呼びかけ、未来への展望や予測、或いは著名人の格言で締めるなどの方法があります。
また再度トピックの重要性を強調する場合もあります。締めくくりに相応しい表現を考えてみま
しょう。

例）In order to come up with a realistic solution we all need to think "outside the box."

4. 挨拶・質問の受け付け（**inviting questions**）

　はじまりの挨拶で築いた聴衆との距離感を保つうえでも、最後に質疑応答の時間を設けること
は重要です。自分の説明で伝わりにくかった箇所などを指摘してもらう機会にもなるでしょう。

例）Now we still have some time left, so please feel free to ask questions.

Language for Presentation

Presentation の Conclusion で使える表現としては、以下のようなものがあります。

1. 主張の繰り返し
   Therefore, …
   Thus, …
   In conclusion, … / To conclude,
   Consequently, …
   Hence, …

2. **Body** の要約
   The main points are as follows: …
   Let me remind you of the issues we have covered.

3. プレゼンテーションの締めくくり
   That's all I have to say.
   That concludes my speech.
   That covers everything I'd like to say.
   Thank you for your attention.

4. 挨拶・質問の受け付け
   Are there any questions?
   Does anyone have any questions or comments?

Vocabulary for Presentation

Exercise A

次の語句の意味を a. 〜 j. の中から選びましょう。

_____	1. cover	a.	意見
_____	2. therefore	b.	思い出させる
_____	3. thus	c.	要約する
_____	4. issue	d.	含む、扱う
_____	5. consequently	e.	結論付ける
_____	6. summarize	f.	注意
_____	7. comment	g.	論点
_____	8. remind	h.	それゆえに
_____	9. conclude	i.	その結果
_____	10. attention	j.	このように／したがって

Your Own Presentation

Unit 10 で作成した Concluding Sentence をもとに、Conclusion の原稿を完成させましょう。

1. 主張の繰り返し：

2. Body の要約：

3. Presentation の締めくくり：

4. 質問の受け付け：

Grammar for Presentation

Imperative Sentences ［命令文］

命令文は、命令だけでなく要求や希望なども表すことができます。主語の You を省略し、動詞の原形から始めるのが基本です。

Look at this figure/table.　Please look at this figure/table.

Don't read from your script.

丁寧なニュアンスの命令文

命令文を丁寧なニュアンスにするためには、Please をつける他にも助動詞を用いる方法があります。

Could/Would you give me more information about that?

Would you mind opening the window?

let を用いた命令文

Let me explain the situation.

Exercise B

次のそれぞれの文の誤りを指摘しましょう。

1. Please raising you hand.

2. Don't sitting down until I say "Thank you for listening."

3. Don't ask him any questions not related directly to the presentation, won't you?

4. Would you mind help me carry these handouts for today's presentation?

5. Let I give you more evidence to support my conclusion.

Exercise C

（　　）内の単語を用いて和文を英文にしましょう。

1. あまり沢山質問せずに、他の人たちにも機会を与えて下さい。（ ask questions / give a chance ）

2. 答える前に、もう少しあなたの質問について考えさせて下さい。（ Let me / a bit ）

3. 最近の選挙については何も聞かないで下さい。
（ Would you mind 〜 ing / not... any / recent election ）

4. あなたの結論を支える何らかの根拠があるなら教えて下さい。
（ Let us / any evidence / you may have ）

5. 講義がとても面白かったので、その人が書いた本を読みたいです。
（ As / lecture / would love ）

Visual aids

　Conclusion は、Presentation の成否を握る大事な部分です。デザイン面にも注意しながら、Presentation 全体の統一感を築き上げましょう。色遣いについては PC 等のディスプレイと印刷物とで大きく異なる場合がありますので、事前にしっかりと確認することが重要です。この課では、色遣いを含むデザイン面についての注意点を学んでいきましょう。

Conclusion で用いられるスライド例

　Conclusion でしばしば用いられるスライドには以下の3種類があります。

1. 主張や理由：1〜2枚程度で、発表で最も言いたかったことを簡潔にまとめましょう
2. 引用文献のリスト：聴衆が同じ情報をたどることができるよう、正確に記しましょう
3. Presentation の終わり：発表が終わったことを示し、質問の受け付けや連絡先を提示しましょう

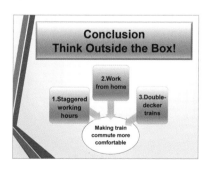

☑ TIPS

◆ **英語の発表に向けたスライドデザインの 8 つのポイント**

・スライドの中の色は、背景色、文字の基本色、タイトルや小見出しなどの色、強調の色の 4 色ぐらいまでにする。

・4 色の使い方には一定の規則性を持たせ、全体を通して一貫した色遣いにする。

・背景色は印刷するときのことも考えて、白を基本とする。

・文字の基本色は、背景色が白であれば、黒やグレーにすると読みやすい。

・タイトル（またはタイトルの背景）や小見出しの色は、落ち着いた色にして、全ページで統一する。

・強調の色は他で使う色とは異なる派手目の色がよい→赤やオレンジが効果的。

・タイトルや強調などで文字の背景に色を付ける場合は、ハレーション（明るい色の組み合わせで目がチカチカする現象）を起こさないように注意する。

・画像やイラストが文字の色と干渉し合わないように注意する。

UNIT 14　Evaluation

これまでの Unit で作った Presentation を自分たちで評価してみましょう。評価の方法は二つあり、自分で自分のPresentation を評価する Self-Evaluation と、クラスメイトの Presentation を評価し、改善点を指摘する Peer Review/Evaluation があります。

Self-Evaluation

> Self-Evaluation では、まず、自分たちの作った Presentation の原稿を以下の Checklist を使って確認します。もし、No になったら、前の Unit に戻って改善しましょう。これを行った後は、想定される質問を考え、リハーサルです。

Exercise A

次の (a) ～ (c) に①～③の選択肢から適当な文を選びましょう。

Checklist for Presentation Structure

Introduction

Did I/we offer a proper greeting to the audience?		Yes / No
(a.	)	Yes / No
Did I/we explain the structure of our talk? (mapping)		Yes / No

Body

Did I/we state our points clearly?		Yes / No
(b.	)	Yes / No
Did I/we provide convincing evidence?		Yes / No
Did I/we provide references?		Yes / No

Conclusion

(c.	)	Yes / No
Did I/we thank the audience and invite them to ask questions?		Yes / No

1. Did I/we use effective signal words/ transitions like "for example"?

2. Did I/we summarize the key point(s)?

3. Did I/we tell the main idea of our talk?

■ Checklist が完成したら、自分(たち)の Presentation 原稿を再確認してみましょう。

> 原稿が完成したら、もう一度読み直してみましょう。Presentation の最後には、Audience から質問を受け付けることも大切な Presentation の一部です。想定される質問を以下に考えてみましょう。

Exercise B

予想される質問とその答えを英語で 2 つ以上考えてみましょう。

[Questions]

1. _____

2. _____

3. _____

[Answers]

1. _____

2. _____

3. _____

Exercise C

次の各文がどんな種類の質問にふさわしい返答か考えて、線で結んでみましょう。複数に引かれる場合もあるかも知れません。質問を想定しながら、なぜそうなるか考えてみましょう。

1. To be honest, I think that raises a different issue.   A. good questions

2. That's a very good question.   B. difficult questions

3. Interesting! What do you think?   C. unnecessary questions

4. Well, as I mentioned earlier,...   D. irrelevant questions

5. I'm glad you asked that.

6. I'm afraid I don't have that information with me.

いよいよリハーサルです。リハーサルを行うのは、英語の発音やことば使いの確認だけでなく、Presentation の内容をしっかり飲み込んでいるかどうかを確かめるためです。特に、英文が自分でも覚えられないくらい長く複雑になっていませんか。Presenter にとって分かりにくい英語が Audience に分かることはありません。

Exercise D

次の Evaluation Sheet は、自分の Presentation のリハーサルでも使い、また、他のクラスメイトの Presentation を評価する時にも使うものです。評価の観点と内容の意味を確かめながら、適当な語（句）を 1〜5 の選択肢から選びましょう。

Evaluation Sheet

Category	Item	Evaluation			
聴衆への配慮 Audience Focus	(a.)	1 poor 2 fair 3 good 4 excellent			
	Interaction (Q & A)	1	2	3	4
内容 Contents	Structure and organization	1	2	3	4
	Clear and logical examples	1	2	3	4
身振り・話しぶり Delivery	Good voice and articulation / Smooth delivery	1	2	3	4
	Posture / (b.)	1	2	3	4
表現・ことば使い Language	Transitions / (c.)	1	2	3	4
	(d.)	1	2	3	4
資料 Materials	Contribution to understanding	1	2	3	4
	Slides	1	2	3	4
説得力 Persuasiveness	(e.)	1	2	3	4
	Benefits for audience	1	2	3	4

1. Evidence   2. Expression   3. Eye contact
4. Signal words   5. Timing and punctuality

Peer Review/Evaluation

> Exercise D で完成させた Evaluation Sheet を参考にクラスメイトの Presentation を評価してみましょう。評価に使う下の図表は、Radar Chart といい、数値をイメージ化し、全体のバランスが分かるものです。クラスメイトの Presentation を評価することは、自分の Presentation の改善にもつながります。Evaluation Sheet に比べて評価の刻み（目盛り）を増やしました。

Presentation No.: ....

Presenter(s): ....

Theme/ Title: ....

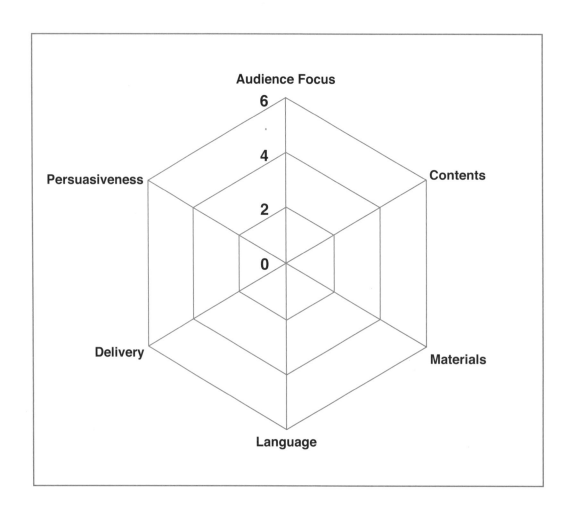

Notes

Appendix

モデルプレゼンテーション原稿

①～⑩の番号は右ページのスライドが表示されるところです。

① Good morning, everyone. I'm happy to have an opportunity to talk to you here today. Let me ask you a question. How many of you ride a train in the morning? Raise your hand. I see. And how many among you have to stand on the train because it is really crowded? Ah, almost everyone. Today I would like to suggest some solutions to overcrowded trains. ② According to a government report, during rush hour, trains in and around the capital are filled to 165% capacity on average, and some lines run at almost double their capacity. Crowded trains are definitely a cause of stress for people in cities, however, there are several ways to make the situation better. ③ In this presentation, I would like to focus on three solutions to this problem: ④ staggered working hours, work from home, and double decker trains.

⑤ My first idea is expanding staggered working hours. This means setting up different working hours for companies located in the same area. For example, some companies' work may start at 8:30a.m., while at others it can begin at 9:00 or even 9:30. Obviously, the end of the working day would no longer be the same for all businesses either. As part of this plan, some companies are already allowing their employees flexible working hours. One company actually offers 13 variations of working hours. Several companies have tried flexible working hours on a trial basis and found out that the employees' commute had become more comfortable, their work efficiency had improved and the quality of their private lives had also improved.

⑥ Another solution is to allow employees to work from home once or twice a week. This way, the number of passengers on trains will decrease. In addition, some people could live and work in a rural area and communicate with the office remotely. Actually, some towns and villages around Japan are inviting people to move there from urban areas, so that they can revitalize local economies. People can enjoy a more relaxed lifestyle in the countryside with no need to use public transit, but still stay connected to their workplace in the city.

⑦ Finally, introducing double-decker trains will increase passenger capacity. Double-decker trains can accommodate over 50% more passengers, so it will obviously be a promising development. In the future, it may be possible to run double-decker trains equipped with doors on both levels by building two-story platforms so that the passengers can get on and off trains smoothly.

⑧ In conclusion, by thinking creatively and implementing innovative policies, we can make the train commute more comfortable for passengers and also improve the quality of life in the cities. Obviously, this is a major problem for millions of residents. We looked at three possible solutions today for the crowded trains: staggered working hours, work from home, and double-decker trains. In order to come up with a realistic solution we all need to think "outside the box." ⑨ Now we still have some time left, ⑩ so please feel free to ask any questions.

①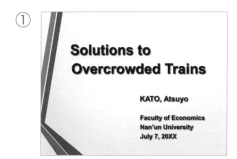

②

③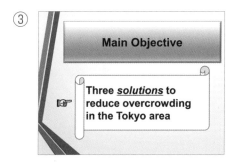

④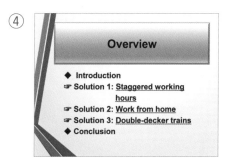

⑤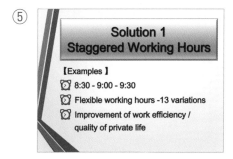

⑥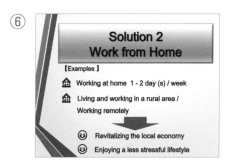

⑦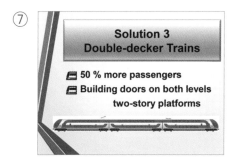

⑧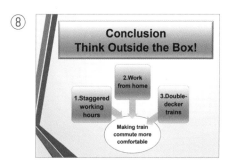

⑨

⑩

Notes

Message Delivered <Intermediate> [B-902]

パターンで学ぶパラグラフ・ライティングとプレゼンテーション入門 〈中級〉

1 刷	2020年3月26日		
4 刷	2024年3月29日		
著 者	レオニード・ヨッフェ	Leonid Yoffe	
	西村 厚子	Atsuko Nishimura	
	奥平 文子	Fumiko Okudaira	
	佐竹 麻衣	Mai Satake	
	森田 彰	Akira Morita	

発行者　南雲一範　Kazunori Nagumo
発行所　株式会社　南雲堂
〒162-0801　東京都新宿区山吹町361
NAN'UN-DO Publishing Co., Ltd.
361 Yamabuki-cho, Shinjuku-ku, Tokyo 162-0801, Japan
振替口座: 00160-0-46863
TEL:　03-3268-2311 （営業部：学校関係）
　　　　03-3268-2384 （営業部：書店関係）
　　　　03-3268-2387 （編集部）
FAX:　03-3269-2486

編集者　加藤　敦

装 丁　銀月堂

組 版　Office haru

検 印　省 略

コード　ISBN978-4-523-17902-3　C0082

Printed in Japan

E-mail　nanundo@post.email.ne.jp
URL　https://www.nanun-do.co.jp/